The Language of Tears

The Language of Tears

David Runcorn

CANTERBURY
PRESS
Norwich

First published in 2018 by the Canterbury Press Norwich
Editorial office
3rd Floor, Invicta House
108–114 Golden Lane
London EC1Y 0TG, UK
www.canterburypress.co.uk

Canterbury Press is an imprint of Hymns Ancient & Modern Ltd
(a registered charity)

Hymns Ancient & Modern® is a registered trademark of Hymns Ancient
& Modern Ltd 13A Hellesdon Park Road, Norwich,Norfolk NR6 5DR, UK

Scripture quotations are from the New Revised Standard Version of
the Bible, Anglicized Edition, copyright © 1989, 1995 by the Division of
Christian Education of the National Council of the Churches of Christ in the
USA. Used by permission. All rights reserved.
Prayers from *Common Worship: Services and Prayers for the Church
of England* (2000), *Common Worship Daily Prayer* (2005) and *Common
Worship: Times and Seasons* (2006) are copyright © The Archbishops' Council
and are reproduced by permission.

British Library Cataloguing in Publication data

A catalogue record for this book is available
from the British Library

978 1 78622 091 2

Printed and bound in Great Britain by CPI Group (UK) Ltd

Jesus said,
'Whoever believes in me...
rivers of living water
will flow from within them.'
John 7.38

Contents

Acknowledgements

Many people have helped the emerging of this book. Particular thanks go to Sheila Appleton, Bishop Robert Atwell, Catherine Benbow, Ian Bussell, Andrew Braddock, Hilary Egerton, Bishop David Gillett, Paula Gooder, Anna Griffiths, Mat Ineson, Tash Kent, Anne Long, Philip Seddon, Fr Silouan, Brother Stuart and Philip Swan for their gifts of time, insight, tears, wisdom and permission to use their stories. Thanks also to the participants in many workshops, training days and discussion groups whose shared insight and experience has enriched these pages.

Very special thanks to Simon Kingston who has once again been a delightful collaborator and tireless guide throughout the book's emerging.

Finally, my thanks to my dear wife Jackie, and to Josh and Leona, Simeon and Kate for coping with a writer in labour. They have been delightful distractions, generously curious and wonderfully supportive throughout.

Thank you to Mike Catling for permission to use his poem on p.18.

With love and thanks
    to Andrew, Ian and Pauline
and all in the Mission and Ministry team
    at Gloucester Diocese.

1

'Tell me about your tears'

I was sitting with a counsellor. I don't now recall the story I was telling but at a certain point tears unexpectedly welled up and flooded all my attempts to continue speaking. I offered the embarrassed apology we feel we must offer at such times. But my counsellor just sat quietly, watching, unhurried. Just letting the tears flow. A box of tissues appeared at my elbow.

And when at last the waters began to subside and I was calming, those were the first words she spoke. 'Tell me about your tears.'

It was an invitation not a question. And that changed everything. Questions like 'What's wrong?' or 'Why are you crying?' demand an answer, yet it may be that *nothing* is wrong. Are tears only for treating as a problem needing to be fixed – like an oil leak under a car engine?

Her invitation unlocked my relationship with tears that day. If she had said 'Tell me about your family', or 'your life', I would have offered her a rambling tour across the varied features of the landscape that forms my personal world. But what she said to me was, 'Tell me about your tears.' I had never thought of tears in this way and I didn't really know how to begin. I was being invited to reflect on a relationship, not to speculate on particular reasons or causes for my tears.

But if I was to tell anyone about my tears I needed first to get to know them better myself. This meant responding to them as more than a physical reflex in the presence of pain or perplexity. At this point I realised I was a stranger to my tears. What might it mean to spend time with them, to listen to them? Perhaps they were speaking to me or I was even speaking through *them* in some way? After all, in my most vulnerable beginnings on earth they were the first and only language available to me. Tears connect us with the deepest part of ourselves and so offer expression to what is far beyond our words and even our thoughts.

In the pages that follow I tell you about some of my tears. Not because they are exceptional. They are not. Nor do I understand all that flows there. It feels like trying to learn a language. Tears go with being a creature who wonders, who longs and who feels things. So I encounter them in moments of joy, pain, bewilderment, wonder, loss and much between. In some situations they are predictable. But they can also be unexpected and mysterious, or puzzlingly absent. My tears reveal something of my character, temperament and life stories. You will find clues here to my emotional maturity or lack of it. I speak of tears as a language, and not simply an emotional reflex, in order to invite a richer engagement with our responses to the whole business of being alive and the ways we experience, understand and express this. So biology, culture, history, gender, chemistry, religion, temperament, spirituality, emotion, literature and feelings all find mention here.

I also write as someone for whom tears have come to have a significant place in my faith, where they find quite frequent expression. At times in Christian history tears have had a central place in the task of discerning, praying and revealing God's purpose and ways. In the earliest centuries, manuals on Christian living paid very special attention to tears and were suspicious if they were not there. The point was vividly made by Isaac of Stella (c. 1100) who wrote:

I am going to tell you something at which you must not laugh, for I am telling you the truth. Though you should suspend yourself by your eyelids before God, do not imagine that you have attained anything in your rule of life until you encounter tears; for until then your hidden self is still in the service of the world.' (Maggie Ross, p. 138)

He also wrote:

When grace has begun to open your eyes, at that time your eyes will begin to shed tears until they wash your cheeks by their very abundance. If anyone teaches you otherwise, do not believe him. To ask of your body anything else apart from tears as an outward sign of reality, is not permitted to you. (p. 38)

This insight has been largely lost in our times and I seek to explore it afresh. But I also hope people of very different faith or none will feel welcome and make their own connections here.

In my exploration, stories of tears have emerged in the most unexpected places. The entrepreneur Duncan Bannatyne is one example. He tells of his tears while doing charitable work among the poor in Romania.

The tears came at about ten o'clock that night. I went outside and found a quiet place at the side of the house. I couldn't stop the tears, my face was wet, my nose began to run and I was a mess. I had no choice but to let the tears flow; and they just kept pouring out of me and wouldn't stop. After

3

many minutes I began to get the feeling that I wasn't alone. It was there and then that God said hello. I felt that I had been consumed by this presence, that something had completely shrouded and taken hold of me. It was unmistakable: I knew who had come and I also knew why. It wasn't a spiritual thing, it was a Christian thing, and I felt I was being told, 'You've arrived, join the faith, be a Christian, this is it.' It was profound, and I stood there, stunned, considering the offer and thinking about what it would mean. I knew I wanted to keep on building up my businesses and I wanted to keep making money, and I also knew I wanted to carry on doing all the things I wasn't proud of – I knew I was never going to be this totally Christian guy going to church on Sundays. So I said, 'No, I'm not ready.' And God said, 'OK', and disappeared. (*Anyone Can Do It*, pp. 230–1)

The tears of many others also flow through this book. They are people of very different character and experiences. Tears are not only for certain types of people, though those who do not find tears easy will find their stories here too. I am grateful for what all of them have shared of their tears and for permission to tell their stories here. On some occasions I have made small changes to details to guard confidentiality. I am aware that tears touch the most sensitive parts of us. It is perilously easy to be clumsy with the feelings and hurts of others. If any are left bruised by what I have written, I am sorry: it was truly never my intention.

At the end of the book I offer three practical resources for exploring tears: 'Tracing our relationship with tears', 'The names we call our tears' and 'Listening to our tears'.

In the ancient cathedral close to my workplace there is a chapel that I love to pray in. On one occasion, with a burdened heart that I knew needed tears to express it, I headed there, hoping to be alone. But I arrived just as a coachload of schoolchildren was preparing to enter the cathedral. My heart sank, as I knew there would be little privacy for the next hour or so. I walked ahead to the chapel and tears flowed strongly. In the background I could hear the unmistakable sound of children drawing nearer so I opted to kneel on the floor against the stone bench behind the altar. I buried my face in the cushion and continued to pray silently.

I began to notice it was unexpectedly quiet. I looked around and found a little boy kneeling beside me, silently copying me. Behind him was a small queue of his friends waiting their turn.

What they saw or understood of my tears that day I will never know. But I treasure the memory and I hope this book offers a similar encouragement to draw near, go exploring and begin to learn the language of our tears. They are part of our relationship with ourselves and our world. They reveal our personal landscape and story – rather like rivers, springs and lakes do in the natural world. Tears are a language rather than just a feeling, but a language we have probably not stopped to listen to before.

2

Living in water

It all begins in water.

In the account of creation in the first pages of the Bible, water covers the depths in the dark and formless void (Gen. 1.1–3). The earliest life on earth evolved out of water. Today the search for life on other planets still centres, in the first instance, on the search for signs of water. Without it we know no life is possible.

Life on this planet continues to be a highly saturated existence. We human beings are made up of approximately 60–70% water. Our brain and heart comprise 73% water and our lungs around 83%. Our skin contains 64% water, muscles and kidneys, 79%. Even our bones are a watery 31% *(United States Geological Survey)*. Like the created world around us water is central in every way to human health and flourishing.

There are practical reasons why our embodied living needs such high levels of fluid. The water within us functions as a shock absorber, cushioning vital body parts on damaging impact. It is vital for our digestive systems. Water facilitates the distribution of oxygen throughout the body. It is needed to enable cells and organs to grow and reproduce and for flushing waste products out of the body. It is essential in assisting the brain in the manufacture of hormones and neurotransmitters. It is also a lubricant throughout the body and the way our body temperature is regulated.

It perhaps should not surprise us that within the fluidity

of our make-up is found a phenomenon called 'weeping' that produces 'tears'. Tears come in three different kinds, each having a different function and role.

'Reflex tears' are the ones we shed when we get dust or smoke in our eyes. They flush the system, clearing out the grit and noxious particles and clearing vision.

'Continuous (or basal) tears' keep our eyes lubricated. These tears contain an anti-bacterial chemical called 'lysozyme' which protects our eyes from infection. Continuous tears also travel through the tear duct to keep the nose moist and bacteria-free.

'Emotional tears' are different again and have further health benefits. While reflex tears are 98% water, emotional tears excrete those particular hormones and other toxins which accumulate during stress. Crying also stimulates the production of endorphins, our body's natural pain-killer, and 'feel-good' hormones. Having a 'good' cry in some contexts means just that – it is good for us. It flushes unhealthy stuff out of our system. Typically, after such crying, our breathing and heart rate decrease and we enter into a calmer biological and emotional state.

Human beings are thought to be the only creatures to shed emotional tears. That alone should alert us that something more than a physical reflex is going on when we are weeping. When we consider that the earliest, most vulnerably formative period of our life was the nine months we spent entirely immersed in water, it may not be so surprising that we communicate through water in a very particular way. There in the womb, before speech or sound was possible for us, movement was our first language. Research reveals that babies move with great sensitivity in response to their mother's changing mood, habits or even *thoughts*; to different kinds of music; to sounds and voices. But upon the breaking of those waters and our birth into this world, our second language was communicated through water.

One of the things that makes tears particularly significant is that they are a point at which our emotional/psychological/ spiritual and bodily selves meet. We are *moved* to tears. Our physical responses can range from a discreet movement of the hand to wipe a tear from the corner of the eye, or something altogether more dramatic – bent over, convulsed or shuddering with tears. But physical tears can be triggered by something we see, the words of a poem, a day dream, a memory awakened by scent or a sound. Tears are a way we express the whole varied business of being alive.

Tears challenge the adequacy of words to express what is going on within us. In fact human communication always involves much more than words. We only accurately receive and interpret words within the much wider interpretative context of sound, movement, facial expression, context, intuition – and guesswork. Only 30% of words are lip-readable. Human communication is always very, well, fluid.

Books that include mention of tears tend to study one aspect or another of the subject. One will analyse the bio-chemical and biological functions. A pastoral manual on bereavement may touch on tears in the context of suffering and grief. But what is often missing is any reflection on their importance for expressing feeling, being aware and for reflecting in depth. Tears have huge significance for how we develop our understanding and consciousness and our search for meaning and purpose in our lives. But discussion or even awareness of any spiritual dimension to our tears is almost totally absent.

Simply because they are a language that has been flowing out of the earliest and most evocative depths of our lives, our relationship to our tears will be complex, mysterious and elusive. A language deeper than words is being expressed here. Through tears our bodies are expressing what is in our hearts. We need to learn how to listen to them.

I have a friend who took his counselling work into partnership with a masseur. He would sit and quietly talk with people while they received massage. Time and again he found that as a patient received caring and attentive touch, memories were unlocked and released, often with tears.

> The body remembers, the bones remember, the joints remember, even the little finger remembers. Memory is lodged in pictures and feelings in the cells themselves. Like a sponge filled with water, anywhere the flesh is pressed, wrung or touched lightly, a memory may flow out like a stream. (Clarissa Estes, p. 198)

Human flourishing, healing and development will always involve, at some point, searching for signs of water. That is what makes life possible.

There are no exceptions to this rule.

3

Gather them

Down through history, and in a variety of cultures, is found the practice of gathering tears and keeping them in a bottle.

There is a poetic reference to this practice in one of the psalms when a struggling pilgrim says to God: 'You have recorded my lamenting, you have put my tears into your flask' (Psalm 56.8; Goldingay, p.175). The psalmist found comfort in the conviction that God too collects our tears and keeps a record of the stories of our pain. Nothing is wasted.

In Victorian England, lachrymatory, or tear bottles, were popular as an expression of mourning for those who had died. At other times they were kept by those whose loved ones were away fighting wars, on the high seas or on other hazardous journeys – a sign of their devotion and the pain of separation. Gathered tears were a way of remembering, of paying attention, of honouring and of being faithful – and an expression of the simple longing to be close to one who was absent.

Some years ago I was the speaker at a conference. I cannot recall the theme. I only remember that at the end of my third and final address I sat down in the midst of the audience and could not hold back tears. I wept uncontrollably. People around were quietly sensitive towards me and there was a scheduled break for refreshments. (It was a conference within the charismatic tradition so this occurrence was perhaps not as startling as might be first thought.) The conference leader, a close friend, took me to a side room. I slumped to the floor and continued to shake with sobbing for some time. How long this continued I do not know. Damp patches gathered on the carpet beneath me.

My friend sat quietly and then as I calmed he remarked in a very matter-of-fact way, 'I can see the angel who is ministering to you. He is collecting up your tears.' The idea that angels were involved at all at that moment was entirely new to me but this was not the time for critical analysis. There was much in that experience I still cannot claim to understand but two things were very clear in that moment. Though totally unexpected, I knew I could completely trust the integrity and authenticity of my friend's insight. And whatever was going on I was being held in an immense, holy compassion.

Tears are gathered in a moving scene near the end of the film *Harry Potter and the Deathly Hallows*. One of Harry's teachers, Severus Snape, is a relentlessly malevolent, ambivalent and bitter character throughout the long Potter saga, with an intense resentment of Potter himself – though quite why has never been made clear. As the final battle with the forces of darkness comes to a climax, Harry finds Snape, terribly wounded and near to death. Harry kneels beside him trying to find some way to comfort him. Tears are flowing down Snape's cheeks. 'Gather them', he says. Harry finds a small bottle and carefully collects the tears. He takes them to a 'Pensieve' – a font-like bowl that in that magical world is a receptacle for containing and revealing memory. He pours the tears into the water and plunges in after them. Snape's most personal and painful memories are now revealed – the socially awkward, lonely young boy, deeply in love with the only person who had ever befriended him – the girl who will become Harry's mother. To add to his pain he is cruelly bullied and mocked by Harry's father and friends. But only now is it revealed that after Harry's mother was killed Snape secretly took on the role as Harry's protector for her sake. But no one could know. It is a story of harrowed, lonely sacrifice and a faithful vigil that plainly nearly broke him at times. Years later when Harry has a son he gives him the second name of Severus. Harry tells him he is named after one of the bravest people he has ever known.

The story was all in the tears. And perhaps it always is. In a poem about her tears a friend prays: 'Lord, collect my tears in your bottle, for each globe holds a world, exposed.'

The photographer Rose-Lynn Fisher specialises in micro-photography. A few years ago she went through a painful time of loss during which tears flowed abundantly. One day she took a teardrop, put it on a microscope slide and photographed it. What she saw was so striking and unexpected that she continued to collect and photograph her tears, noting as she did so what particular event triggered them and what feelings accompanied them. The images have a stark simplicity and beauty. Many look like aerial reconnaissance drawings in pen and ink, with landscapes and coastlines and even settlements. The scenes vary enormously across expressions of loss, joy, bewilderment and pain. No two tears are alike. And onion tears, by contrast, make a totally different image. They resembled frost on a window pane.

Fisher's tears became for her a way of reflecting on her life that was as creative as it was evocative.

Tears are the medium of our most primal language in moments as unrelenting as death, as basic as hunger and as complex as a rite of passage … It's as though each one of our tears carries a microcosm of the collective human experience, like one drop of an ocean. Wordless and spontaneous, they release us to the possibility of realignment, reunion, catharsis:

shedding tears, shedding skin. (*The Topography of Tears*, pp. 7–8)

Like streams and rivers across the countryside, tears may be found flowing in, around and through our human story, welling up like springs in the midst, shaping the contours and stories of our lives as they do. They are part of an essential irrigation system for our growth and fruitfulness, softening the ground of our soul where it has become hard and downtrodden and, like springs, soaking it all with extravagant exuberance.

Tears trace and shape the personal landscape of our lives and reveal its character.

They have to do with love.
They help us remember.
Tears are for gathering.
They are not for wasting.
God does not waste them either.

4

For those with no tears

Not everyone weeps.

Others do, but with painful difficulty – like tightly wringing out a cloth for a very few drops, or even like shedding blood.

Some simply cannot weep. Tears are not there to be shed.

In one of his poems, Michael Symmons Roberts recalls a voice early in his life – perhaps a parent – telling him not to cry. 'Lachrima negativa' is a dry-eyed lament over the fact that he has not been able to cry ever since. He is aware of times when tears are welling up in his depths. But he pictures the spaces behind his eyes as like the heavily silted flats of a river estuary. His tears are all absorbed there, sucked into the ground. They never flow out (*Dysalter*, p. 113).

There is no one reason why tears may be absent. In an age when pious tears were greatly stressed, the saintly Christian pastor Richard Baxter struggled with his inability to physically weep over his sins until it was wisely suggested to him that he had 'a Nature not apt to weep' (Alec Ryrie, p. 192). While there are some, like Baxter, for whom tears are simply not their most natural response, there are others for whom the lack of tears may be a sign of wounds or hurts that need care and healing.

A woman working in the business world reflected on the hardening effect that a competitive, driven environment can have on our emotional expressiveness. But she continues: 'I am not a weeper. I learned early that crying doesn't accomplish anything, and it could expose a hope within me that was likely

to be dashed. If I made myself vulnerable to another, I could –
and would – be hurt.' (Center for Action and Contemplation).

A childhood memory comes to mind. I was walking home with
my mother. Across the hall from our flat was a pram and in it a
baby was crying loudly. I remember asking my mother why no
one came, because the baby was so upset. 'He has to learn not to
be selfish,' she said. That was the prevailing child-rearing theory
of the day. To cry, to demand a response and expect people to
come running, was self-centred. This had to be trained out of
children – by ignoring them. The actual reason for the tears –
hunger, cold, pain, fear – was not considered relevant.

But what was a helpless, four-month-old baby expected to do
in its distress? Learning not to be selfish is a very adult concept
and implies choices that babies can neither grasp nor exercise.
Is it not more likely that what that child was learning was that
when it cried out in need no one would come? Its tears – the
only language it possessed – were in vain. And we might wonder
in what ways that experience laid the foundations of that child's
personal and emotional development for living.

One reason tears may not come is that we have learned
they are hopeless. When we cried, no one came. So we stopped
crying. This is a form of what psychologists have called 'learned
helplessness'. It refers to what happens when our repeated
attempts to seek the comfort or help we need continue to elicit
no response and eventually we simply give up trying any more.

In one of the rare contemporary books on prayer to include
a discussion of tears, Richard Foster acknowledges those who
cannot, or who struggle to, weep. He himself is one of them. If
this is you, he says, do not be discouraged. The ancient guides
would agree: 'I judge toilers by their struggle, rather than their
tears, and I suspect God does too,' says John Climacus (Maggie

Ross,p.160). But both insist tears are something we should continue to seek and to pray for. Yet it has to be said that Foster's advice does sound rather judgmental towards those who do not weep, as if they are in some way hard-hearted or resistant.

These are some of his suggestions, but I have softened his wording (from *Prayer*, pp. 46-7).

If tears are not present or are a struggle to express:

1   Be gentle and uncondemning with yourself. There may be significant reasons for this.
2   While noting the advice to Baxter, beware of simply assuming you are 'not the emotional type'. Human personality does not come typecast like that. As we have seen, non-emotional responses may have been *learned*. If we are unaware there may be other possible responses within us we will easily assume they are not there and that 'this is me'.
3   'Immerse yourself in the Gospels,' says Foster. They draw us close to the character and presence of Jesus – one so fully alive in our joys and pains. The image of immersion is helpful. If parts within us have become dried out or even hardened, a good soaking in God's compassionate presence is a way to soften them.
4   Where there are no tears outwardly, we can shed them 'inwardly', in intention. 'Have a weeping heart even if your eyes are dry' is the advice (p.46). A lack of tears on the surface does *not* mean you do not feel and care in the depths. It needs to be emphasised that if you are one for whom tears are few *you are not less compassionate*.
5   Pray for the 'baptism of tears'. Jesus teaches, 'Ask, and it will be given to you' (Matt. 7.7). (Prayer, pp 46-7

I would add three further reflections on the experience of what some call 'dry tears'.

6   Some people who do not otherwise shed tears, weep in their sleep. This can be a natural, psychological response or a gift of God's Spirit. I recall waking once with a clear memory of having sobbed my way through a difficult dream in my sleep. I then remember lying in bed feeling unusually refreshed, as if a weight had been lifted off me.

7   Isaac of Stella knew of this phenomenon as a gift of the Spirit and counselled tearless people going through painful struggles to simply go to their room and sleep 'until the hour of darkness passes from you'. He tells of some who wake with their bedclothes soaked from tears shed as they slept. (Maggie Ross, p.167).

8   If tears are hard to find, and we sense we need them, we may need to do some exploring. Is there a struggle or resistance going on? Are there prohibiting voices? If so, what are they saying? We may be drawing near to vulnerable experiences or wounds in our lives that have deeply shaped our responses – including our capacity to feel and to shed tears. At such times the loving discernment of others may be helpful. (I offer some resources for exploring this in the appendices at the end of the book.)

Tears

My life is held in these teardrops
gathered within but seldom shed.
They hold all that I feel and all that
I am or may ever want to be.

I cannot trust myself to weep
for fear of being washed over
the cliff edge and becoming
nothing but a water fool.

Jesus wept, but I cannot unless
a pet dies or a moving scene in
a play or film touches something
unnamed that lies deep within me.

I feel this deepness like a well
inside my soul, the bottom of
which I cannot reach even if
I lower myself down in the dark.

I would not have wept at the
tomb of Lazarus, but only for
his dog, if he had one, left
wondering where his master was.

God of Tears soak my soul
and well up within me
so that rivers of living water
flow out into the parched land.

Mike Catling

*(A meditation by someone for whom weeping is not easy.
It was inspired by a training day for spiritual directors on the
theme of tears, led by David Runcorn.)*

Bowl of Tears – a prayer exercise

Here is a suggestion for personal or group prayer that gives symbolic expression to tears that are not physically there to be shed.

Take a clear glass bowl. Pour water into it.

Let the water represent our tears for the world and all life.

Place the bowl of water in the centre of the group. Invite each person to come forward as they choose – more than once if they wish. They may stand, sit or kneel before the bowl, scooping up some water and letting it trickle through their fingers.

They may wet their face or eyes with the water to represent their tears. As they do, they may say, silently or aloud:

'My tears are for. . . .' (name a person, place or situation).

At the close of the prayer time together, invite each person to offer a word or phrase that expresses their desire and intention.

(Center for Action and Contemplation)

5

Our emotional orbiting

The Soul of the Night is the story of Chet Raymo's personal pilgrimage as an astronomer and physicist. It is passionate, poetic and deeply felt but he begins in a very unexpected place. 'Yesterday on Boston Common I saw a young man on a skateboard collide with a girl' (p.3). She was flung into the air, bounced twice as she landed and lay still. For a moment all was silent. How does Raymo respond? The astronomer kicks in. He describes how in the few seconds the girl is in the air the turning world pulled her half a mile to the east, the motion of the Earth around the Sun carried her 40 miles westward and the galaxy of the Milky Way carried her 300 miles on its orbiting circle. And then she hit the ground.

Raymo takes the emotional shock of the incident into intellectual orbit around the stars that fill his professional life. Feelings are there but displaced. We often do this. But from the distance of stars he is trying to respond. That silence is what disturbs him – as does, it becomes apparent, the deep silence of space. He is wanting to hear something. 'I turned the volume of my indignation all the way up, and I heard nothing.' Pain, tragedy, meaning and randomness are all the big themes implicit in a story like this. What kind of world is it where such things happen? Raymo feels it deeply – 'My heart thrashed silently in my chest.' But what noise did he expect and from whom, in that moment? Who was he indignant with? And why was his own reaction to thrash *silently*?

Oddly, we are never told if the little girl survived.

Simply because our emotions and feelings flow from such powerful, vulnerable and deep responses within us, we do not easily experience them directly. There are defences at work. In Raymo's story, as in ours, a revealing and concealing goes on at the same time. He is feeling deeply but copes with the demands of the story before him by creating a narrative of his own with which he orbits around it.

Listening to the language of our feelings and tears involves detective work. One of the places to start is to notice where our tears surface most readily, comfortably or even enthusiastically. For some this may be a piece of music or line of poetry. It could be nature or art. Certain scenes in literature or film may be a trigger. For others it may be in a passionate identification with the varied fortunes of a sports team or celebrity. But even as we clutch our tissues it may still not be obvious what it is that is touching our depths.

A friend writes:

'I find tears enormously difficult to receive: I think I've only cried between ten and twenty times in my adult life. I've often wished I could cry more easily, as I always feel much better when I do. However, there are things in films which I watched as a child which do set me off (*The Railway Children* being a typical one), but I don't count these as 'tears' in the fullest sense.

I quoted his words in a workshop for spiritual guides. What might this story be revealing about his tears, I asked them? How would you explore it with him? The response was slow, so I asked, 'What scene in *The Railway Children* do you think he might be referring to?' One of the group flung her arms out and cried, 'Oh daddy, my daddy!' The emotional response in the room was immediate – even those who had not seen the film.

Set in Edwardian, pre-war England, this classic children's story tells of a comfortably well-off family whose happiness is shattered when their father is wrongfully arrested and imprisoned. The reasons are never clear. The family are forced to move to a run-down cottage out in the country, close to a railway line. It is a story of childhood innocence, of the loss of a parent, of sustaining home and hope in difficult times, and the awareness of a shadowy adult world that is neither safe nor fair. But in the famous last scene at the end of the 1970 film version, Bobbie is on the station platform as a train comes in. Clouds of steam shroud the platform. It is impossible to see anything. The train pulls out. The steam slowly clears – and, suddenly, her father is standing there. 'Oh daddy, my daddy!', she cries, and runs and flings herself into his arms.

My friend speaks of struggling to *receive* tears. This is much more than saying 'I cannot cry'. The language suggests an offering or gift that, for whatever reason, he has been unable to accept and make his own. So in one sense he is right. The tears shed over a film scene are not 'real', but they are connecting with personal stories or memories that *are*. This is an example of the way that our emotions take these indirect routes and attach to unsuspecting things to talk to us. Frederick Buechner writes:

You never know what may cause them. The sight of the ocean can do it, or a piece of music, or a face you've never seen before. A pair of old shoes can do it. You can never be sure. But of this you can be sure. Whenever you find tears in your eyes, especially unexpected tears, it is well to pay the closest attention. They are not only telling you something about the secret of who you are, but more often than not God is speaking to you through them of the mystery of where you have come from and is summoning you to where, if your soul is to be saved, you should go to next.

From our earliest years our imaginations are fed on stories that express the gifts, threats, dilemmas of the world we are growing into. They tell the dramas of love, tragedy, good, evil, hope, despair and much between. The repeated themes in our folk stories are ones of long-lost identity, of wicked spells and entrapment, and of longing for release and transformation. All those ugly ducklings who are really beautiful swans; the grotesque toads who are actually handsome princes; ragged kitchen maids who will become the king's true love. All waiting for the kiss of one whose love is true, to break the spell, to change the world and to reveal who we truly are.

For this we weep, in the waiting and the longing, with our dreams of another story, waiting to be told.

6

The tears of a priest

I do not remember anyone telling me, when I began ordained ministry in the Church, that it would be a calling to tears. But it has been.

Without warning they began on my ordination retreat. I wept through the entire time with a turbulent mixture of terror and awe, grateful for the care and support of the retreat leader. I have wondered ever since what he thought this incoherently soggy heap on the floor in front of him was doing on the threshold of ministry in the Church of God. Tears have accompanied my ministry journey ever since.

I regularly speak to groups of men and women who are involved in various expressions of Christian ministry and reflect with them on their experience of it. On one occasion I offered an unplanned aside, saying, 'As we have been reflecting on all this I would not be surprised if tears have been close to the surface for some of you.' I went on to speak about both the costliness of ministry and of the neglected place of the gift of tears in the life of Christian discipleship down the centuries. I began to notice some movement as I spoke. Some were discreetly reaching for tissues. Afterwards a number of people sought me out, moved and excited, wanting to talk about their experience of tears in ministry and prayer. Few had discussed it with anyone before. None had ever heard that it might be a gift rather than a (less helpful) part of their own personal, emotional make-up that they assumed reflected negatively on their capacity to cope. Since then I have regularly spoken of tears in that context and there is always a strong response of recognition. In conversation afterwards a typical comment is, 'I have always cried easily but had no idea it might be a gift of prayer or sign of the Spirit in me.'

When it comes to our relationship with our more vulnerable but expressive emotions a certain rule applies. Unless there is somewhere we have heard these responses affirmed as normal, appropriate and even a gift, and unless we have known ourselves accepted, loved and respected when they have been present, we will tend to assume the truth is the opposite. We will assume they express weakness or are an indulgence and we will respond with embarrassment, shame and even anger with ourselves. If they surface too publicly we presume the need to apologise for them.

Those outside the more formal catholic traditions of priesthood and ritual worship will probably not have heard of a maniple. It is one of the vestments a priest is expected to wear when celebrating communion. It looks like a wide bookmark and is worn over the left arm. We know of its use in the Western Church from the sixth century onwards, though it was certainly around a lot earlier. But what was it for?

It most likely originated as a handkerchief worn by Roman men in the heat of the Middle East, to wipe the dust and sweat of the day from their faces. A heavily robed priest in that climate would surely need the same. Over time, as the rituals of worship formalised, the maniple became as ornate as the rest of the priestly garments.

But it seems the maniple once had another, very practical, use. Before the service each item of priestly vesting is put on with a special prayer. The clue lies in the words the priest prays as the maniple is put on. 'May I deserve, O Lord, to bear the maniple of weeping and sorrow, in order that I may joyfully receive the reward of my work.' The need for a cloth to wipe the face is more than sweat – it is to wipe the tears that flow in the offering of sacrifice and joy that is the heart of Christian faith and discipleship. A guide to priestly duties written in the eighteenth century by Alphonsus de Liguori spells this out: 'It is well known that the maniple is for the purpose of wiping away the tears that flowed from the eyes of the priest; for in former times priests wept continually during the celebration of the Mass' (Grimm p. 217). In the Roman Catholic Church the maniple was an obligatory part of the vestments for the Mass until in 1967 it was decreed that 'the maniple is no longer required'.

I have a friend who is a minister in a local church of a more informal tradition. Mat Ineson tells of how tears accompany him in his public ministry and he is learning to listen to them when they surface:

'They come when I am not expecting them, often when I am speaking about or reflecting on the love of God, or speaking about forgiveness and grace. I used to think it was an expression of passion in me, or something that is touching me, and it may be that. But sometimes it seems to come suddenly and often it seems to release tears in others or add to the message that I am speaking. Sometimes it is a reflection of joy, sometimes of pain or lament, sometimes of repentance. It particularly happens while speaking about unconditional love or when I am simply aware of the delight of God's presence. In general it may happen when I'm leading worship, preaching, or when I am just present. I have more recently taken it to be a sign that the Spirit is at work in the community and in me. At such times I will now invite people to come for prayer. The most powerful and memorable experience was at a previous church when I was trying to lead a service where we were reflecting on the joys and pains of the past twenty years including the deaths of the previous vicar's wife and several others dear to the community. There was a release of grief that came through me as I read the stories and this in turn released things in others. It was so strong that I couldn't carry on and someone had to take over, even though I didn't really know the people involved.'

A maniple – or at least a good supply of tissues – is still required.

7

Men, women and tears

A collection of poems was published a few years ago, chosen by a number of well-known men. Edited by Anthony and Ben Holden, it was called *Poems that Make Grown Men Cry*. I understood why. They were beautiful and very moving. But it was the word 'grown' in the title that stood out. This is the stubborn old stereotype that tears are something men grow out of. It takes something exceptional to make *grown* men cry.

It is true that in British culture the expression of tears is more readily associated with women than with men. But what is to be gathered from this is quite another matter. Research shows that women weep four times as often as men in UK society. But it is less well known that this is explained in part by the fact that the tear glands of men and women are anatomically different. And instead of labelling women as more emotional we might be curious as to why men do not cry more.

I incline to the view that discussions about emotions that focus on gender-specific behaviour serve no one well. There are societies, including my own, where men are strongly conditioned to hide vulnerable feelings. But in other cultures around the world no such assumptions are made. In one of the very few books about tears written from a Christian perspective, both women and men share their stories. But the interpretation of men weeping is that they are 'discovering their feminine side'. This book, *The Blessing of Tears*, quotes often from the

Bible without noticing that no such gender-based distinctions are made there and that its crowded pages are full of men who, among other attributes, are able to weep freely and without embarrassment.

I bring to this discussion my own upbringing as a boy growing up in a patriarchal society. I attended a single-sex school where male identity was characterised by loyalty to the team and where hierarchical authority, toughness and competition were stressed as character-building. There was a suspicion of one's feelings, a despising of weakness and even a hostility towards women. In that world there was a terror of being thought feminine or weak in any way. Men could only touch each other affectionately or express vulnerable feelings if they had first hit and insulted each other. Sensitivity was to be concealed. Poetry or art was only acceptable if it was *very good*. As most of our attempts were not in that league, we learned not to risk the mockery of our peers. The male role-models of my childhood were heroic (often masked) loners – fearless, tough, sexually irresistible, able to save the world, but quite incapable of expressing sustained, relational intimacy of any kind. Feelings were therefore a matter of vulnerable anxiety. Often violence was a way of expelling what could not be expressed any other way. To a significant degree I entered adult life with my most formative thoughts and feelings unexpressed within and therefore unexplored.

There I grew to recognise that a male identity which prizes toughness and requires the repression of emotions is actually bad for men. In the UK, suicide is presently the highest cause of death among men under 45. The reasons are varied but the problem is compounded by a male culture where it is difficult to talk about or express vulnerable feelings. 'Man up' was a campaign in Australia where, as in the UK, men are three times as likely to commit suicide as women and the rate is rising. To speak into a highly macho culture the campaign used film of men crying and emphasized what a positive and helpful thing it was to express and speak about their feelings. It also sought to teach friends and colleagues how to respond and care when people needed to do so.

Women, like men, must make their own journeys through the powerful social messages that shape our responses to our feelings. In work and business environments, traditional male requirements of restraint can still determine what is considered acceptable behaviour when it comes to the expression of emotions. Those who shed tears are likely to lose respect or are assumed to lack resilience. In a moving personal reflection on her working life, JoAnn Shade notes how many twenty-first-century women have embraced the mantra 'Never let them see you cry' in their world of work and have done so without being able to acknowledge the cost to themselves. She learned the same was required while in senior national roles in her church, and she duly worked hard to stay in control of her emotions 'to avoid appearing weak or overly feminine'.

It takes considerable mutual trust if feelings are to have a positive place in collaborative working environments. Good intentions are not enough. In my experience church and faith communities may not be any easier places to achieve this than any other. The senior leadership team in a Christian organisation recently crafted a 'work covenant' to articulate the core values on which to base the team's working relationships and approaches to decision-making. It included these statements:

'We will risk sharing our feelings with each other.'
'We will speak directly and honestly to each other.'

I write this shortly after a much-loved colleague in my workplace died of cancer. Despite long treatment and the prayers of many, there came a day when we gathered in the office to hear the news that her cancer was no longer treatable and that she did not have long to live. We were already a close team but in our common grief we shared words and feelings as we had not done before. The next day two of the men in the team were thanked for their tears as that had made others feel it was alright to cry.

No two journeys towards human expressiveness are alike. We are all shaped in different ways by the gifts and constraints of culture, community and our personal stories. In these we are, more than we know, sources for each other's binding and releasing.

After many years on one track, JoAnn Shade's career changed direction. A different work environment offered her the challenge of loosening her well-learned emotional restraints and to thaw the 'ice maiden' she felt she had become. Tears began to surface.

> Old habits are slow to die, and I often find myself attempting to squeeze them back, but they've been persistent, leaking out, ambushing me with ferocity, when I least expect them. I am gradually coming to accept a real woman who can both weep and laugh, who can plumb the depths of sorrow but also claim the fullness of joy that Jesus described as 'like a river, overflowing its banks' (John. 16.14, *The Message*), 'immersed in tears, but always filled with great joy!' (2 Cor. 6.10, *The Message*)

When I read that story as a man I ask myself how I would express my own aspirations to be a fully feeling person.

8

The language of life

I completely misheard a passing comment over the breakfast table and made a response of baffling irrelevance. A puzzled glance. A realisation. And we just slowly dissolved, clutching tissues as we went. For several minutes we were just weeping with laughter.

A good laugh is as cathartic as a good cry. My ribs ached for half the morning.

Tears are a language for the whole of life not just the grieving or 'serious' bits of it. They accompany any and every mood and experience of life from our highest joys to our deepest desolation, the trivial to the most profound. So our relationship to tears is a reflection of our capacity to be fully alive and living, deeply and expressively. Our capacity for joy is also in direct relation to our capacity for grief. The social restraints all too commonly placed on tears of grief are at work in all our other emotional responses too. Avoiding sadness takes a lot of energy. Company that tends to push away negative subjects or 'sad' stories will tend not to be obviously at home with happy ones either. Forced laughter is not funny. It is a defence mechanism.

When someone begins a journey in counselling or with a spiritual guide there is usually a presenting reason – a question or a problem the person is seeking help with. But as the exploring deepens it can often be accompanied by a loosening of the boundaries of feeling and behaviour. Within a trusting relationship, away from familiar social restraints, without the need to be polite or to protect the feelings of others, a whole variety of emotional responses may begin to stir and surface. This is not without some embarrassment, for it is not the polite and 'acceptable' side of ourselves that emerges at such times. It can be very unsettling to discover the depth and power of expressiveness that is in us. There may be outbursts of anger, tears, joys and a range of unsettled and fluctuating moods between. With this can also come feelings of exhaustion. We will often have been holding lids on our depths for some time. The first task is to receive all this, to listen to it, and to begin to make a relationship with it. It is, after all, ourselves we are meeting.

Robert Macfarlane writes on the themes of landscape, nature and the particular way in which human identity and memory abides there. He is concerned at the way contemporary living is mediated and manipulated more and more through artificial image and technology, so we are increasingly distanced from our physical world. We experience life by extension and are no longer in touch.

> There has been a prising away of life from place, an abstraction of experience into different kinds of touchlessness. We experience, as no historical period before, disembodiment .... We have in many ways forgotten what the world feels like. We have come increasingly to forget that our minds are shaped by the bodily experience of being in the world ... its spaces, textures, sounds, smells and habits. A constant and formidably defining exchange occurs between the physical forms of the world around us and the cast of our inner world of imagination. (*The Wild Places*, p. 203)

There are times when God chooses to shock church and

world into awakening. A feature of spiritual revivals in church history are the bodily and emotional responses that accompany them. Manifestations vary but they typically include quaking, trembling and falling to the ground as well as emotional outpourings of tears, groaning, laughter and excitable cries of worship and prayer. *Everything* awakens up in the presence of God. It is chaotic, often controversial and frequently criticised as childish. But it is first and foremost a sign of life.

Child*like* describes it better. The unsophisticated Pentecostal awakenings that still continue around the world a hundred years since their first beginnings, have been described as restoring the gift of play to an over-serious, grown-up Church. Jesus himself said, 'Unless you change and become like children, you will never enter the kingdom of heaven' (Matt. 18.2–3). One of the features of the religious leaders who opposed Jesus was their relentlessly wooden seriousness and the underlying edge of anger that always accompanied them. Jesus likened them to moody children in the marketplace, impossible to please. 'We played the flute for you; and you did not dance; we wailed; and you did not mourn.' (Matt. 11.17).

In his song, *My true feelings*, Graham Kendrick wrote of an awakening of the life of God in him:

> Now I can laugh I can cry and I can sing
> The sweetest joys and saddest tears can now begin
> An honest heart and honest eyes
> – it's been a beautiful surprise –
> Since God gave me my true feelings.

There is a sense of release in these words. An *authentic* life is now possible. I do not know what he refers to, but the word 'honest' comes twice in these lines and with a sense of clear relief. For

Kendrick, this awakening has freed him from a certain kind of pretence, the need to 'perform' in a certain way in order to be acceptable. The effort of sustaining a required image is draining. The reference to *'true* feelings' acknowledges that our passions, moods and impulses can and do mislead us. They can be misdirected. But if our emotions are a problem it is not because we have them in the first place. It is that they are not fulfilling their true purpose and gift in us.

This sense of awakening is not dependent on outward circumstances. After all, the most extraordinarily privileged people can be bitter and miserable, while profound joy can be found in the midst of pain and poverty. The 13-year-old Anne Frank describes a moment of finding herself intensely, almost unbearably, alive within the shuttered rooms where she and her family had been hiding from the Nazis for over two years:

Today the sun is shining, the sky is deep blue, there is a lovely breeze and I'm longing – so longing – for everything. To talk, for freedom, for friends, to be alone. And I do so long … to cry! I feel as if I'm going to burst, and I know that it would get better with crying: but I can't, I'm restless, I go from room to room, read through the crack of a closed window, feel my heart beating, as if it was saying, 'Can't you satisfy my longing at last?' I believe that it is spring within me, I feel that spring is awakening, I feel it in my whole body and soul. It is an effort to behave normally, I feel utterly confused. I don't know what to read, what to write, what to do, only that I am longing. (*Diary of Anne Frank*, p. 130)

The first and only gift is life. If we are to speak its language we must simply immerse ourselves in the messy, haphazard, unpredictable business we call living.

9

Companionship of creation

She is standing in torrential rain, weeping. 'I'm sad because it's raining,' she says. 'It's raining because you're sad,' her companion replies, with ponderous seriousness. The conversation drowns in its own meaninglessness, typical of the quirky, nonsensical exchanges that made *Men in Black* such an entertaining film.

But in so many ways the created world does shape, echo or minister to our varying moods and needs. How is it that a walk in the countryside can totally lift my spirits? I return to life with a new perspective, but my life itself has not actually changed. The raw power of the sea or winds can leave me feeling empowered and invigorated. The constant popularity of the breath-taking documentaries about this amazing planet Earth underlines this. For all our capacity to sentimentalise or shamelessly exploit it for our own ends, the created world continues to have a way of meeting and touching us deeply.

In the Bible, creation has its own life in God. It has, of course, been around much longer than us. 'Where were you when I laid the foundation of the earth?' says God to Job (Job 38.4). And the Bible's vision for our saving and transformation is not just for humanity – it is cosmic, a new heaven and earth. We are constantly reminded that we are part of something so much bigger. Creation is not just there to meet our needs.

In the poetic imagination of the Bible, creation exuberantly participates in the worship of God. Mountains, seas, trees, animals and birds are all pouring out their praise – singing, shouting, clapping their hands, night and day. 'Their voice is not heard' (they are without human speech), but 'their voice goes out through all the earth' (Ps. 19.3-4). We can be prone to very sentimental responses to creation but I still have a vivid memory of taking a boat journey down a river in the Amazon a few years ago. I became increasingly aware of music. The river was singing. That is the only way I can describe it. A continuous, harmonised flow of celebration as strong and alive as the river itself. It was full of joy. I trailed my hand in the water in wonder and wept for the honour of being allowed to hear it.

In a mysterious passage, St Paul describes creation also groaning with longing frustration as we wait for the fulfilling of God's salvation in the world (Rom. 8.22). Creation, after all, bears cruel scars on account of the human capacity for exploitation and destructive living.

I have also known what I can only call the compassion and companionship of creation.

Some years ago I was in deep personal crisis. I was burned out in work and faith and close to a breakdown. With the help of friends I spent some months abroad and then two months alone in an Alpine cabin in Switzerland. It was a relief to be alone. I was aware that my life had become over-identified with my public identity. I needed to know who and what was there if none of that drove my life any more. The first unexpected thing that happened was the weeping. Tears became my language. There in the solitude they replaced words. I was on my way back from the edge, and day by day there were moments of light and darkness, joy and pain. On one particular day I sank into a place of deeper darkness. I spent a long while slumped on the floor, weeping. I felt very lost and frightened. There is a not uncommon fear that if we start weeping we might not be able to stop. How long I stayed there I do not know, but slowly the flood tide receded and the tears stopped. I was still with that mixture of numbness and heightened awareness that can often follow a strong outpouring of grief. I became aware of the old log stove in the corner of the room behind me. It was a familiar crackling and clunking, while the leaky old kettle on top hissed and steamed. It had the feel of a wise old friend who loved and understood but would not intrude upon this moment by coming nearer. I became aware of the bare plank walls of the cabin around me. I felt their shelter and security. But they too watched without closing in upon my space. I lifted my head and looked out of the window. Below, the pasture grasses were swaying on the steep meadow slopes in the evening wind. Above and beyond, the clouds were tugging on the snowy mountain peaks and I felt the cooling air of approaching night. Everything around me seemed to understand. There was no anxiety. All around me knew a secret. It was not for telling. All I knew was that I was held in reverence and love.

More recently, I was on retreat with a group on the ancient pilgrimage island of Bardsey, off the north-west coast of Wales. We started each day in a chapel together, and something in the prayers one morning awakened an ache of pain in me for the Church and all it was facing, including my own longing and perplexity in it.

As I walked away from the chapel I tried to talk about it with a friend. But I began to feel physically sick with the weight of tears within. I have had such times before. I knew the only thing I could do – the only thing necessary – was to find somewhere alone and let it all pour out. I stumbled into the nearest meadow and for the next half- hour I simply wandered in deep grief, little understanding what was going on, offering it all to God, without knowing in what way or how this might be praying. But I sensed it was.

I do not know when the weeping stopped. When I came to myself I was standing quietly looking out to sea. The storm had passed. I felt calm and at peace and slowly became aware that all the while a breeze of indescribable gentleness was brushing across my cheek. It felt like a caress. There on that island, in the early light, on the winds of the morning, I again knew myself loved in creation with infinite tenderness.

10

Sign and symptom

The service was interrupted by loud and unrestrained bouts of weeping and wailing. The woman was notorious for this. It would frequently happen in church worship, but on other public occasions as well. The tears came and went without warning and were often prolonged. It was disruptive and caused embarrassment. There were suspicions of mental instability and attention-seeking. But there was also the resentment and envy that strong religious fervour can attract. Here was an uneducated, illiterate woman behaving as if she had some privileged, superior relationship with God that by-passed all the ministrations of the priestly hierarchy of her day.

Her name was Margery Kempe. She was born in Kings Lynn, Norfolk, around 1373. She was tried for heresy several times, violently persecuted, suspected of being possessed by the devil and was sternly reminded that St Paul forbade women to preach. All we know of her is found in *The Book of Margery of Kempe*. It lays claim to being the first autobiography in the English language and it was probably dictated to her son and a local priest.

There are features of her story and faith that remain controversial and difficult to interpret. But she was a fearless, forthright and feisty personality who stood in awe of no man (and it was men who confronted her) and plainly gave as good as she got. It would be interesting to consider how a local church today would cope with behaviour like that.

Kempe had a severe mental breakdown after the birth of the first of her (14) children. But it would be a mistake to look there to explain her subsequent behaviour. She did not weep during her illness. Her recovery began when she received a life-changing vision of Jesus, which was the beginning of a passionate and intimate devotion that consumed the rest of her life. Now the tears began to flow – a response to the love she met in Christ. Key to her healing was her escape from the severe stress on sin taught by her spiritual guide, and from his imposition of hair shirts and other physical punishments masquerading as Christian devotion. In the vision, Jesus assured her of his love for her, that she was forgiven and that she should cease these practices. So to understand Kempe's weeping we must look to theology not psychology. This was a gift of tears.

It is their sheer quantity and the attendant noise level that make Kempe's tears stand out. She herself found her wildly demonstrative weeping unsettling and she struggled to understand what was going on. She had no control over the tears. It was as if someone was turning a tap on and off inside her. She even begged in prayer for them to stop, but this was not granted her. Jesus appeared again in a vision in which he explained the meaning of her tears. They were, above all, an outward sign of Kempe's deep and passionate love for Christ. They were also an expression of penitence and sorrow for sin – though without getting into the destructive self-negation of her past state. Confession of sin led to the grace of forgiveness and new life.

Far from being an expression of a self-absorbed piety, her tears were a dramatic, outward witness to Christ and his loving presence in the world. They were also a willing sharing in the sufferings of Christ for the sins of the world. So her tears were both an evangelistic and a prophetic sign to those around. She prayed at length, and by name, for others to be drawn to the same faith and salvation. Her book records God thanking her that because of her story 'many a man shall turn to me and believe therein'.

Throughout her life tears came and went at the will of Christ, to whom she was utterly devoted. They thus expressed her complete dependence on God and her willing submission to his will and purposes in and through her. Kempe comes to be grateful for this rather difficult blessing. Her understanding of her tears as a symbolic and public gift sustained her whenever they drew hostile attention, as they frequently did.

There may be parallels in the Pentecostal tradition, which is the fastest-growing church in the world today and is often found among the poorest, most vulnerable and least educated communities in society. It too attracts mockery and persecution for its more demonstrative manifestations under the unpredictable movements of the Holy Spirit. It too knows of the gift of tears. But something called the gift of tongues (a prayer gift of an unlearned language inspired by the Spirit) occupies a special place in that tradition. The Orthodox theologian Kallistos Ware has noted the similarities:

> 'Speaking with tongues' seems to represent an active 'letting go' – the crucial moment in the breaking down of our sinful self-trust and its replacement by a willingness to allow God to act within us. In the Orthodox tradition this act of 'letting go' more often takes the form of the gift of tears. (*The Orthodox Way*, p. 101)

There may be a further connection to be made between tongues and tears. When given to illiterate, marginalised and voiceless peoples of the world, tongues are a liberating gift of eloquence – an unlearned, fluent language inspired by the Spirit; a gift of prayer and worship to those who previously had no voice or status in the world or church. Walter Hollenweger suggested that the symbol and sign of tongues 'is to restore the power of expression to people without identity and power of speech, and to heal them from the terror of the loss of speech' (*The Pentecostals*, p. 459). Perhaps, Kempe's tears may be seen as a subversion of the social hierarchies of her day, ignoring the performances of the respectable; by-passing social and verbal controls and undermining the cherished presumptions of male, political and priestly priority. In this way 'tears release us from the prison of power and control and into the vast love and infinite possibility of God' (Maggie Ross, p. 38).

Contemporary movements of the Holy Spirit typically include demonstrative manifestations like shaking, falling helplessly to the floor, laughing, groaning or weeping. They are similarly mocked or criticised. But when one person was interviewed after spending an extended time helplessly shaking on the floor of a large, packed auditorium he was asked what God had done for him there. 'He took away my dignity,' he replied. But he said it as if this was an immense and liberating relief.

Weeping itself was not exceptional behaviour in the Catholic Middle Ages. 'Pious weeping' was familiar as an expression of devotion and penitence and actually encouraged in the devotions of the faithful. This carried over into the Protestant Churches of the sixteenth century, taking examples from characters in the Bible. So the true Christian 'weepeth bitterly with Peter, or nightly watereth his couch with tears, as David' (Alec Ryrie, p.187).

If to modern readers this torrent of tears down through

history seems bizarre or extreme, Kempe and others would surely wonder how our eyes stay as dry as they do before the love of God.

11

Streams in the desert

I had been leading a workshop on the Christian desert tradition of life and prayer. In the third and fourth centuries, significant numbers of men and women rejected life in the newly Christianised Roman Empire and 'fled' to the desert wastes of the Middle East and North Africa. They were compelled by an urgent need to seek God. They knew there were things to renounce radically. They believed this world needed mourning and repenting over, deeply. ('Weep! Truly, there is no other way than this', was a typical saying (William Harmless, p 239). But they were not abandoning the world for some escapist dream. What they sought was a new way of living and praying faithfully in the world. Everything was at stake. The desert needed water. They watered it with their tears.

A man came up to me afterwards, moved but distressed. 'You could be describing my office environment,' he said. 'It is a desert. We were once a team. Now it is all competitive. There is no heart to what we are doing any more – just relentless targets and pressure for results.' Others joined the conversation with similar stories. Jesus himself observed, 'What kind of deal is it to get everything you want but lose yourself? What could you ever trade your soul for? (Matt. 16.26, *The Message*).

David Whyte, the international work consultant and poet, speaks and writes extensively on these themes. In his book *The Heart Aroused*, he explores the task of 'melding soul life with work life, the inner ocean of longing and belonging with the outer ground of strategy and organizational control'. He urges the need to go beneath the 'surface concerns' about growth and profits and to address 'the needs of the heart and soul, and the fears and desires' that the working environment too often requires us to keep hidden.

> The severest test of work today is not of our strategies but of our imaginations and identities. Our lives take the form of an absence. We become exhausted from the effort needed to sustain our waking identities. The day may be full, we may be incredibly busy, but we have forgotten who is busy and why we are busy. We lose the conversation. We lose our calling. Everything is at stake, and everything in creation, if we are listening, is in conversation with us to tell us so. (*Crossing the Unknown Sea*, p.60)

These are turbulent and uncertain times. Most organisations are under immense pressure to reinvent or re-invigorate themselves. In response to the challenges a particular corporate persona has tended to lead the drive for growth and change in business and institutions. The result is that initiatives for change tend to prefer extroversion and to value 'precision more than vision, systems more than people, and structure more than flexibility' (Leslie Francis). This is not without positive impact, but a drawback can be the lack of relational and emotional suppleness needed for working effectively with the people and communities most impacted by the change.

A friend and leadership consultant writes of the present context:

It is easy to panic. The strain to get some results, to turn some tide, is enormous. Even when we have read up on the analysts, sociologists and the organisational theorists, is there still something we don't know we don't know? Something that would allow us to wait in the ruins with patience, equanimity, faith and hope?

In any system under huge pressure for results, an organisation will too easily assume that if a chosen strategy is not working it is because we have not been working hard enough or using the right method. The public face of the organisation will be upbeat and positive, while the emotional life at its heart will find no room for expression. The cost to morale and relationships in the affected communities may be very high.

John Kay is one of the leading economists in the United Kingdom. In his book *Obliquity : why our goals are best achieved indirectly*, he traces a significant shift over the last 40 years in approaches to business and finance in the UK and beyond. Prior to this, business mission statements routinely emphasised the product not the profit as motivation. There was an explicit belief that if the product was good profitability would follow – and indeed it generally did. Why does this sound so naïve now? Sony Corps' first mission statement included the line 'we shall eliminate any unfair profit seeking'. The shift has been to the explicit goal of increasing profitability. In industry generally, the product has become increasingly incidental. One of the investors in the Dragon's Den went unchallenged when he mocked a would-be inventor for forgetting that 'the main purpose of it all is to make money'.

But Kay offers numerous examples that show how this strategy has never been good for the well-being of a company as a workplace or as an employer. It invariably results in shorter- and even longer-term *loss* of profitability. We just don't work well or efficiently this way. Profitability is a by-product of other factors. It is a spin-off. So Kay argues that real life is oblique. We achieve our goals by approaching them indirectly. He calls this 'obliquity'.

> Obliquity is necessary because we live in a world of uncertainty and complexity; the problems we encounter aren't always clear and we often can't pinpoint what our goals are anyway; circumstances change; people change and are infuriatingly hard to predict; and direct approaches are often arrogant and unimaginative. (*Obliquity*, p. 24)

Kay argues that an oblique approach to growth will be a process of experiment and discovery, improvisation. It is humble in the face of complexity. We flourish in indirect responses. An oblique approach is reflective, intuitive, including of affective gifts and emotionally nurturing. We cannot ignore this without paying a high price in terms of anxiety, stress, driven-ness, insecurity and grief.

In our times we too need another way.

We need streams in the desert.

12

Resilient tears

The rewards are great for anyone in our society who can identify those human qualities that will guarantee to make the difference and turn everything around towards growth, flourishing and profitability. And because that search is always elusive we live in anxious and unsettling times.

For a sustained period there has been a focus of attention on 'leadership'. But the interest has been turning, out of sheer necessity, to a quality called 'resilience'. The word is to be found everywhere and the reason is obvious. The relentless pressure for performance and productivity has come at the price of human well-being and flourishing. Every year millions of working days and billions of pounds are lost to stress-related issues including those in the workplace.

Meanwhile yet another series of *The Apprentice* has been shown on television. Once again the winner has been rewarded with a lucrative business partnership for their resilience in fighting their way through a prolonged exercise in which various candidates have shown shameless and ruthless self-promotion, public betrayal and criticism of colleagues, unprincipled ambition, wildly unsustainable business vision and – perhaps most importantly – the avoidance of any critical self-reflection. Tomas Chamorro-Premuzic and Derek Lusk's study of leadership appointments in the business world observes that those who are resilient enough to reach the top of their chosen profession may have achieved this by training out of themselves precisely those qualities of leadership the business most needs if it is to flourish.

When the word 'resilient' came up in a discussion group I attended, it was clear that many could only hear it as a demand to 'toughen up'. This suspicion is not without foundation. I once went to an organisation to propose the creation of regular facilitated support and reflection groups for all who worked there. It was a medium-sized business but with a highly stretched workforce that was showing clear signs of stress. Such groups have been used to real effect in similar organisations elsewhere, yet the discussion was curtailed and the proposal turned down by the chair who expressed the concern that if you encourage people to share their problems they will only end up having more. The proposal was treated as an indulgence that would undermine the resilience that the task needed. When the demands of our own resilience leave us unable to empathise and support the resilient journeys of others, the price has surely been too high.

But resilience is not about toughness; it is about suppleness. It is the ability to be flexible under pressure. The resilience we need is the ability to bend and flex back under life's varied pressures. It is the process of adapting well in the face of trauma, stress or tragedy. Resilience is not developed by excluding our emotional vulnerabilities – quite the reverse. If we remain tough and refuse to bend, we become brittle and may break.

Resilience is learned and developed. We are not born with it. Nor is it a quality given to a heroic few. Everyone is resilient in his or her own way. We have all already developed strategies for those times when we are under pressure or life makes hard demands of us. There is much to admire in the way people cope with pressure, pain and adversity. But not all ideas of resilience are helpful.

Resilience is a word borrowed from physics where it describes a material's capacity to absorb energy under mechanical stress and return to its normal form when the stress is released. If stress is too great, the material will deform permanently and eventually break. The appropriateness of this word at all for speaking of human endurance and well-being is at least questionable. 'Resilience's descent to humans from mechanics is not helpful. Humans aren't like steel rods – we are tender, complicated creatures, and words affect our hearts more than we know' (Jarral).

Research into the mental and emotional well-being of soldiers who have been exposed to prolonged stress and danger reveals two strategies for coping. Significantly, those who emerged with the greater degree of personal integration and emotional health were not those who had been toughest in the field, without apparent need of help and support. In fact those who had toughed it out in that way often had greater difficulty adjusting to the next stage of life, and if they did break down their recovery was far less certain. It has been said that 'overused strengths become weaknesses'. But those who clearly felt the pressures, who showed vulnerability and expressed feelings, who could ask for support when they needed it, and who sometimes had to withdraw for a time when things got too much, they were the ones whose resilience led to a greater relational and emotional health in the longer term.

Above the cliffs of an area of North Devon where I used to live, trees must grow under the constant pressure of the strong winds off the sea. They develop a distinctive curve, bending inland with the prevailing wind. They appear to have developed a resilient strategy in a rugged climate. But it can come at a cost. They can only move in one direction. If the wind ever changes direction they will have no response to make, no flexibility. And on one dramatic night some years ago that is exactly what happened. A fierce wind came down the valley and simply snapped the tops off all those trees.

For many, our society is one in which winds are now blowing in *all* directions.

Developing resilience in such a world is a both/and process. It requires allowing yourself to experience the strength of your feelings and responses – but also learning to recognise the times when it is important to continue to function *without* showing or expressing them. There is 'a time to weep,' the Bible says (Eccles. 3.4), and a time to *refrain* from weeping. When I went through a very tough time at one stage in my professional life a key to my surviving was the support I found in a counsellor I saw once a fortnight. Those sessions provided a very necessary pressure release. I could weep and rage, and I did. But it was also a space where I was helped to listen and reflect on what was happening and how I was responding. My resilience slowly grew. It was raw and vulnerable but it enabled me to move from grim endurance to something unexpectedly creative.

Resilience grows as we are willing to step forward, lean into and actively engage with the problems before us. But this is not through avoiding distress or suppressing emotion. If resilience requires a closer engagement with stress and adversity at times, we will also need the wisdom to know when to step back. We need an awareness of what the situation is taking out of us and what our limits are. We will need to know the times and spaces for our recharging and re-energizing. There is a right self-love in such moments which is very different from self-indulgence or cowardice.

Resilience that leads to flourishing is not the tough endurance of a heroic loner. It is not good to be alone though there are times when that is part of what we are facing (cf. Gen. 2.18). Healthy resilience requires the nurture of human warmth and relationships and the support of those who love and know us. And it is within a nurturing community that we are enabled to stand alone.

Resilience is a gift learned in the wrestling and struggling with life. It is forged through our fiercest and most vulnerable tears.

13

'Water the earth'

My wife has a memory from early childhood. She came downstairs early one morning and found her father sitting in the lounge. He was weeping. 'Why are you crying?' she asked him. 'I'm just praying,' he said, as if no other explanation were necessary. She came to realise that tears often flowed when he was praying. I doubt he had heard of 'the gift of tears', but he did not need telling. Nor did he attach any special status or significance to them. As he always did, this humble man was faithfully saying his prayers before the family awoke and he went to work. In the evangelical tradition the heart of prayer is intercession – praying *for*. And as he prayed for the world and its needs, tears flowed.

'Praying for' is an instinctive response in the midst of a world of such painful and complex needs as ours. I suspect we do it whether we own a particular belief or none. Jesus constantly encouraged people to pray out of simple trust in God's loving goodness and intention. 'If you then, who are evil, know how to give good gifts,' he said, 'how much more will your Father in heaven give good things' (Matt. 7.11). Praying is not trying to make God do something he does not want to. God does not need persuading to love us. Nor does God need briefing on what we need at any particular time – and some intercessions can sound suspiciously like that. God is present and active before we even begin to pray. He invites our participation in his love for the world.

In Christian worship 'the intercessions' are the point in the service where the needs of the wider world are named and offered to God. But interceding means more than 'speaking on behalf of'. It literally means to 'stand' or 'go' (*cede*) 'between' (*inter*). This is where Christ is found. It is the place of the cross. Intercession is costly work and so much more than a list of prayers and needs. It requires a willingness to imaginatively enter the world's anguish and pain *for its own sake* and there to cry and wait in yearning love. We must be willing to grow beyond the kind of prayers that simply circle around personal needs, or are poorly concealed bids for special favours. All our loving, like our religious language, needs a kind of sanctifying.

The task is to learn to live where Jesus lives, and pray as he prays. It can often be a place of tears, and where they flow they may be expressing different things.

This is well illustrated by the experience of a participant at a training course in spiritual guidance. She offered to be the 'guide' to a 'pilgrim' sharing her story, while others observed. What was shared was unexpectedly harrowing and related in unsparing detail. As she listened, tears began pouring down her cheeks while the pilgrim telling her story was dry-eyed throughout. At one point the pilgrim stopped to ask her if she was all right. She was, she said, and reflected later: 'I felt as though I were a divided person – two people in one. Tears of pain and despair in one while the other was at peace, calm, listening and speaking a few words to highlight what the pilgrim was saying and feeling.' At the end of the session the pilgrim said she had been unable to express any emotion throughout the ordeal she had described – she was numb, frozen. She said to the guide, 'You have cried the tears I could not cry and your tears have been a great release for me'.

To pray for others and the world is an obligation for all people of faith. But some have a particular calling to intercessory prayer and they illustrate for us something of what it means. Rees Howells taught that there were three marks to this kind of prayer: identification, agony and authority. They are, of course, the marks of the crucified Christ. They remind me of a priest I knew on a very deprived estate. She had those marks upon her. Whenever she talked of her community she wept. But with her vulnerable identification came an undeniable authority of spirit.

In the Eastern Orthodox tradition, Staretz Silouan is remembered for his intercessory prayer. But he would have added a fourth mark to Howell's list: 'glory'. In a rare insight into intercessory prayer Silouan tells of praying for a young Russian migrant worker – one of many forced by poverty to leave his family and seek seasonal work at the monastery where Silouan lived as a monk.

> In the beginning I prayed with tears of compassion for Nicholas, for his young wife, for the little child, but as I was praying the sense of the divine presence began to grow on me and at a certain moment I lost sight of Nicholas, his wife, his child, his needs, their village, and I could be aware only of God, and I was drawn by the sense of the divine presence deeper and deeper, until, of a sudden, at the heart of this presence, I met divine love holding Nicholas, his wife and his child and now it was with the love of God that I began to pray for them again, but again I was drawn into the deep and in the depths of this again and again I found the divine love for them.' (Simon Barrington-Ward, pp. 73-5).

Tears of intercession were well known to the spiritual writers in earlier centuries. Our prayers flow from an awakening of love that flows out into all things.

> A sign of the working of the Spirit within you consists in the kindness which represents within you the image of God, through which, when your thoughts extend to all people, tears flow from your eyes like fountains of water, as if all people were dwelling in your heart, and you affectionately embrace them and kiss them. Your heart is kindled with the power of the working of the Spirit within you as with fire. (Charles Mingana, pp. 165-7).

A prayer that begins in vulnerable human need ends in the depths of divine love. It always does. An unexpected seam of glory and joy has a way of surfacing in writings on intercession. In a very moving moment at the climax of Dostoevsky's novel *The Brothers Karamazov* a central character, Alyosha, is granted a vision in which all comes together – heaven, earth and everything:

> Alyosha stood, gazed and suddenly he threw himself down upon the earth. He did not know why he was embracing it. He could not have explained to himself why he longed so irresistibly to kiss it, to kiss it all, but he kissed it weeping, sobbing, and drenching it with his tears and vowed frenziedly to love it, to love it forever and ever. 'Water the earth with the tears of your gladness and love those tears,' it rang in his soul. (p.104)

14

Poise

Every year a woman called Hannah came to the shrine to worship with her husband and with his second wife and her children. But Hannah was childless – or, as this ancient story tells it, 'the Lord had closed her womb' (1 Sam. 1.5). There was no deeper pain for a woman in that culture. The narrator here is stating the fact of the situation rather than suggesting judgment. Not surprisingly Hannah finds these annual visits unbearable and she sits alone while others feast.

But on this particular year something happens. We are not told what triggers it. The moments in which we tip from passivity into action are rarely predictable. But Hannah is suddenly decisive. She gets up and goes and presents herself before the Lord. All restraint gives way and she pours out her grief to God with deep shuddering tears. Watching at a distance is the old priest of the shrine. He assumes she is drunk and rebukes her in the crudest language. She protests that she has not been drinking but is praying out of deep distress. He brusquely blesses her prayer and wanders off. But her prayer is answered; her womb is opened. Some years later she returns, bringing her son, Samuel, to the shrine. The old priest is still there. She goes up to him. 'Oh, my lord... I am the woman who was standing here in your presence, praying to the Lord. For this child I prayed; and the Lord has granted me the petition that I made to him' (1 Sam. 1.26–27). That is a very gracious spin on what happened that day. 'Standing' is the usual English translation here and the Hebrew word can also mean 'standing ready'. Although 'poise' is not a common translation I follow Robert Alter in using it here for two reasons. Firstly, it heightens the contrast between Hannah's overwhelming grief and the way she later recalls herself in that moment. The use of 'poise' rather than simply 'standing' also directs attention beyond her physical posture to her faith, which is utterly focused on God. To be poised usually describes a graceful equilibrium. So it is an unexpected word to use of someone so racked with grief she was assumed to be drunk. Weeping is more usually described as a loss of poise or composure and being 'beside ourselves' rather than being self-possessed.

'Poised' also describes someone focused, alert and ready to respond. And this is the emphasis in this story. Although Hannah is plainly harrowed with grief, every description of her suggests purposeful, directed faith. The phrase 'before the Lord' is repeated four times in this story. Whatever others around are seeing and assuming, Hannah describes herself as poised before God. She will not be silenced. She has gathered everything of her story - her yearning pain, the heart of her longing and faith - and holds it, passionate and poised, before her God. She has not fallen apart or broken down. Has she ever been more balanced? She knows that if God is the source of life and blessing then it is to God we must bring the perplexity and anguish of life's struggles.

Hannah's story opens the long saga of Israel's history called the book of Samuel. Her story is often told as a kind of affecting domestic tale that explains where the (real) actor and leader in the story came from. In fact Hannah's poised faith, and her journey from barrenness to life, provides the interpretative key to the whole story.

In the only other place where this word is used in the long saga Alter again translates it 'poised'. The boy Samuel is now serving the Lord in the Temple as Hannah had promised. In the night the Lord comes and stands 'poised' over him as he calls him to his service (1 Sam. 3.9–10; *The David Story*, p.17).

In her tears of poised, directed faith Hannah mirrors and perhaps even models God's poised presence and purpose over our lives.

15

The tears of God

Traditional Jewish belief teaches that Moses himself received and wrote down the first five books of the Hebrew Bible – the Torah – from God. But there is a practical problem with this. Moses' own death is recorded before the end of the last book. There, we read, his life was taken 'at the command of the Lord' (Deut. 34.5). The literal translation is 'by the mouth of the Lord'. The Talmud teaches this to mean God took the life of his servant Moses with a divine kiss.

In the first book of the Torah, Genesis, human life had begun as an intimate gift of life breathed from God's own mouth into the earth creature's nostrils, 'and the human became a living being' (Gen. 2.7; Robert Alter, *Genesis*, p.8). The Torah closes with God withdrawing his breath from his creature, also at the touch of his mouth. For the Talmud this is a way of describing life that begins and ends in divine, compassionate gift – a breath and a kiss. But that still leaves the question as to how Moses wrote those last verses, having just died. The answer? 'Up to this point the Holy One dictated and Moses wrote, and from this point [Moses' death], God dictated and Moses wrote in tears'. (Nehemia Polen, p.86). This is a highly allusive and poetic way of reflecting on these events. But what does it mean? Was Moses weeping as he wrote or did he now continue to write with tears instead of ink? And whose tears were they? Nowhere else through his long and eventful life is Moses to be found weeping.

There is a strand of interpretation that suggests that the last verses of Deuteronomy were written with the tears of *God*.

> The only God known to Jews is the God who has poured himself onto parchment, who so loved his servant that he wept over the creature's death and by weeping, disclosed his own implication in finitude. Tears are the only disclosing solvent for the Absolute ... The capstone of the Torah is the Divine weeping. (Nehemia Polen, p. 86)

This is a hauntingly beautiful thought. The work of creation and God's continued self-revelation and presence within it is completed through God's own tears.

The Bible is quite unembarrassed about speaking in humanly physical and emotional terms to describe God's presence, character and activity. And this adds a particularly intense, passionate intimacy to the relationship of God to his world and his people described there. This is a God who speaks, hears, reaches out, remembers and touches. God is variously described as being 'near' and 'far from' his world and people. Of course the Bible does not believe God literally has physical hands, eyes or a larynx. Nor is he more in one place than another. God is Spirit and God is Life. The surrounding nations are regularly mocked for worshipping their idol gods as physical realities. It is one of the things that distinguishes the God of the Hebrews from the gods of the surrounding nations, that the God of the Hebrews *cannot* be seen.

The God whose life sustains all things and holds them in being is variously to be found laughing, grieving, loving, furiously angry, gently comforting or just silently present. He feels deeply and passionately about the world and his purposes within it. He commits himself in covenant relationship to his people. He cares and longs for all he has made and when it goes wrong this hurts and grieves him. As he surveys a world descending all too soon into wilfulness, sin and chaos before the flood, God speaks of his pain, using the same word that describes Eve's pain in childbirth and Adam's toil at work, in their life in exile from the garden of God's delight. The same word is used when God speaks of his pain that the kingship of Saul, Israel's first king, has not worked out and must be replaced (1 Sam. 15.11). God tells his people through Jeremiah, 'my eyes run down with tears night and day, and let them not cease', as he grieves over their pain and tragedy (Jer. 14.17). When his people prove faithless, as they often do, he speaks with the broken-hearted anguish of a marriage partner abandoned for another, but unable to forget the one he loves. He seeks out his beloved, longing to re-kindle the first love once again (Hos. 2.2 and 14–15).

Jesus taught that to see him was to 'see the Father'. So we meet the unseen God, through a human being full of deep and passionate feeling – joy, pain, anger, frustration and more. Jesus is often described as groaning. The word suggests a sound out of his very guts and it must have been quite distinctive. He groans from his rawest depths in the presence of human death, pain and brokenness (John 11.33). This could be in angry frustration, sheer theological frustration or out of the personal isolation of what he knows and bears in the midst of the ignorance and opposition around him (Mark 8.12). On the cross he cries out in the terrible anguish of abandonment.

Jesus' ministry was often expressed through tears. The book of Hebrews tells of times he was heard praying 'with loud cries and tears' (Heb. 5.7). Although he will shortly raise him from the dead, Jesus weeps by the grave of his friend Lazarus. On another occasion he weeps as he looks over the valley to the city of Jerusalem (Luke 19.41–44). In another wonderfully tender image he speaks of his longing as like a mother hen unable to gather and protect her wilful and wayward young (Luke 13.34–35). He grieves for the tragedy he knows to be coming upon the city.

In Bach's St Matthew's Passion, Jesus wrestles alone and in terrible anguish in the darkness of the Garden of Gethsemane as he contemplates the path to suffering and death. He comes to the place of final surrender and self-offering singing these words, 'If my tears be unavailing, take the very heart of me. That my heart … a very chalice be.'

There is, in the heart of God, a chalice of tears.

Life given, restored, sustained on the breath, the kiss and the tears of God.

This is the way God loves.

16

The wholeness of God

That God feels for, is moved by and weeps over this world is such a commonly expressed belief and prayer that we would be surprised by the suggestion this was in any way questionable. But from the early centuries of the Church and for the greater part of church history, the belief that God experienced such passions was believed to be heresy. This is called the 'doctrine of impassibility' – the belief that God is above human emotions and vulnerabilities and cannot be changed by them. An emphasis on an all-victorious and invulnerable God shaped the content of this teaching too in a European Church that for centuries grew under the patronage of dominant military and political powers.

The doctrine of impassibility was increasingly challenged through the twentieth century and in the light of the Holocaust it became unsustainable and simply offensive to many. The image of a God who is dispassionately ordering the world, distant and unfeeling in the face of such horrors, is surely blasphemous in the light of human history. And does not the cross suggest the opposite? Depictions of Christ's suffering on the cross in Christian art and in films like *The Passion of the Christ* became ever more harrowing and explicit. The doctrine of impassibility was blamed on the influence of Greek Stoic philosophy on early Christian theology.

It is surely understandable that we should be reluctant to attribute to God something as unstable and shifting as human emotions. But impassibility is an easy doctrine to misunderstand. It never meant that God is without feelings. Rather, this doctrine teaches that God is not subject to the *unreliable* emotional passions and unpredictable mood swings so familiar in human living. He does not, for example, erupt and act in violent, irrational ways. This is surely good news. It is also significant for many who struggle in the presence of strong emotions. One of the more common stories of tears shared by those I have listened to in the preparation of this book is the memory of the power of early experiences of unpredictable and coercive adult emotion (usually that of a parent) in the life of a vulnerable child. These experiences can and do mean that, throughout life, encounters with the strong feelings and emotions of others are experienced with an undertow of fear and insecurity. So it will not be immediately obvious to everyone that a God who feels deeply and strongly is one who can be trusted in the midst of our own vulnerabilities and needs.

Some human emotions can be called non-cognitivist. We experience these like reflexes. They can be random and unpredictable, triggered by things like fear, anger or pain. They can come and go in a rush. Their expression may not be in any proportion to what has triggered them and we may feel powerless to control them when they surface. 'I *lost* my temper' is a good description of what happens at such times. A repressed response, like a moody sulk and withdrawal, *is just as strongly emotional.*

Cognitivist emotion, by contrast, is a response based upon an actual judgment or attitude I have come to about something. It involves no less 'feeling'. Deep emotion may be present but I am not driven by it. What I feel is part of a wider response to a situation involving my mind, will and actions. Might this be a way of expressing how God feels in the fullness that is his being?

God has perfect emotions, affections not passions, because his value-laden judgments are true and accurate ones. God's love, jealousy, wrath, compassion, and kindness are involved judgments, ways of 'seeing' with the heart that inclines him towards action of some sort but do not overwhelm him. They do not incline him towards evil and they cannot sweep over him because they are fully-consonant with his perfect knowledge and will.' (Derek Rishawy)

There is a question that still needs to be answered. What makes a feeling, suffering God good news? How does such a God change or even save the world rather than just comfort or empathize within it? Putting it bluntly, don't we need a God who does more than weep with us? It is certainly comforting to read in the Bible that we have a 'sympathetic high priest' who knows and understands our weaknesses. But importantly the passage goes on to stress how Jesus did not give in to temptation as we do (Heb. 4.15–16). Jesus did not come just to 'feel our pain' but in order to end it.

This is where we need to rehabilitate the doctrine of impassibility. The good news of God in a world like ours is precisely that he is *not* like us. God is not under compulsion in relation to us or his world. No one and nothing forces his response. He is free and acts out of freedom towards us. In a famous passage in the letter to the Philippians Jesus reveals his likeness to a God who does not cling or grasp. Instead he freely empties himself to enter this world (Phil. 2). The one who knew no suffering in himself willed to become as we are without being overcome by what overwhelms us. Even at the cross Jesus lays down his life – he allows himself to be handed over: his life was not taken from him (John 10.18). He hands over his spirit at the point of death (John 19.30). The suffering of an impassable

God opens the way to a new way of living and loving. That is why the title of a study on the doctrine of impassibility so helpfully speaks of 'the creative suffering of God'. 'To affirm God's impassibility is to confess that God's action in Christ is nothing other than the beautifully gratuitous outpouring of his invincible, unsurpassable, enduring love for his wayward creatures' (Derek Rishawy).

A small number of people in society experience life as *synesthetic*. This is a condition where words, shapes, concepts and sounds are simultaneously experienced with other sensory responses like smell, colours or flavours. For example, the jazz musician Duke Ellington saw notes in colour. The D note was a dark blue burlap, while a G was light blue satin. One person describes her experience of this interrelating of the senses as being like creating 'a certain definite architectural structure in her mind's eye' (Andy Draycott). The result is, to varying degrees, an experience of life whole.

I play with the thought that this offers a way of imaging how God loves and feels in the life and passion that is his. And through the gift of his creative suffering among us he invites us into the same fullness – passionately alive and in full colour.

17

Protest

Jesus was once invited to a meal at the home of a Pharisee called Simon (Luke 7.36–49). There were a number of such occasions in the ministry of Jesus. They often became highly controversial and this meal proved to be no exception. Jesus had been locked into wearyingly familiar arguments with his opponents. 'Wisdom is justified by her children,' he sighed, enigmatically. The wise know what all this means.

Meals in that culture were public occasions. Around the edge others would be watching and listening to the conversation. The presence of one person in the crowd would certainly have caused a stir. A local woman was there. She is not named but the story strongly suggests she had been deeply touched by an earlier encounter with Jesus. Luke's description of her as an 'immoral woman' sets up the contrast with Simon and his guests who presume their own goodness. But until you have reached the end of the story it is not apparent what has been going on.

As Jesus reclines at table, the woman, overcome with love and devotion, kneels and repeatedly kisses Jesus' feet, washes them with her own tears and anoints him with oil. Jesus knows that Simon is revolted by this and is judging Jesus for allowing this woman to touch him at all. There is both the issue of her immoral reputation and also the scandal of public intimacy. Then, as now, this scene would cause considerable embarrassment. What we had not known is now revealed when Jesus confronts his host. It seems that from the moment he had arrived Simon had subjected him to a series of calculated, public snubs. In spite of being an invited guest he had been given no water for washing on arrival, no customary kiss of greeting and no anointing with oil.

We can imagine the woman watching all this going on with mounting anger and distress. She now intervenes. With her kisses, her tears and her oil she publicly reverses all the affronts of Simon. In the absence of a towel she even lets down her own hair to dry his feet. For a woman to let down her hair in public was scandalous. That intimacy was only for offering within the privacy of the marriage relationship. But not only is Jesus unembarrassed, he gratefully receives 'this sweet fragrance of excessive love' for the gift it is and contrasts it with the loveless behaviour of his host (Sarah Coakley, p.5)

Once again we have a Bible story of tears with a quite unexpected outcome. This is highly emotional behaviour that by most familiar social standards would variously be judged excessive, publicly inappropriate, lacking relational boundary and even suggesting personal instability. But it is not only welcomed and received by Jesus, it comes to stand as an angry, prophetic protest that simultaneously reveals who Jesus is and judges the insulting behaviour of those who oppose him.

Her tears are wise.
She is a child of Wisdom.

By the rivers of Babylon
Four reflections on Psalm 137

By the rivers of Babylon —
there we sat down and there we wept
    when we remembered Zion.
On the willows there
    we hung up our harps.
For there our captors
    asked us for songs,
and our tormentors asked for mirth, saying,
    'Sing us one of the songs of Zion!'
How could we sing the Lord's song
    in a foreign land?
If I forget you, O Jerusalem,
    let my right hand wither!
Let my tongue cling to the roof of my mouth,
    if I do not remember you,
if I do not set Jerusalem
    above my highest joy.
Remember, O Lord, against the Edomites
    the day of Jerusalem's fall,
how they said, 'Tear it down! Tear it down!
    Down to its foundations!'
O daughter Babylon, you devastator!
    Happy shall they be who pay you back
    what you have done to us!
Happy shall they be who take your little ones
    and dash them against the rock!

18

Sitting

First reflection on Psalm 137

There we sat down and wept (Ps. 137.1)

Sometimes sitting down is the most important thing we can do.

In a friendlier world, letting people sit down is a gift of hospitality and welcome to arriving guests. 'Welcome! Come on in and have a seat,' we say. But the scene in this psalm is very different. They sat down by the rivers of Babylon because that is where their forced march ended. Perhaps soldiers stood around them, mocking them, in the pitiless heat of the day. A foreign power had laid waste to their land, destroyed their Temple and razed their holy city to the ground. Those not slaughtered were beginning life in servitude in a far country. This was more than a military or political defeat. It was a theological catastrophe. It seemed even their God had been defeated by foreign gods. On those riverbanks we can imagine the full enormity and tragedy of what had happened overwhelming them.

There they wept.

Sitting down is a very sensible thing to do when you find yourself in a strange place. It is even more essential when life is in turmoil. Sitting still is vital because we need a point to start from. If we are going to get anywhere we need to start from *some*where. Physically sitting down and being still is the most practical way of becoming present to who and where we are.

From this place will emerge the discernment of how and in what ways we may respond to what is going on. But first we must just stop. At such times tears will often flow. They may be part of our arriving, expressing what the journey has demanded of us, or perhaps a grieving over what has been left behind. But here we are. And although, as for the psalmist, this may be the last place on earth that we want to be, the first thing asked of us is an acceptance of the present.

There have been documentaries on television in recent years where cameras have followed groups of women and men as they join in the life of a monastery or convent for a week. Most have no previous religious experience. We are first introduced to them in the midst of their wildly active, endearingly chaotic, contemporary lives. We hear them express their hopes and feelings about this experiment. We then follow their journey to the monastery door and into a strange land utterly unlike their own (see Monastery in the references at the end of this book).

There they sat down.

The first thing they encountered was not God, the monks, or deep spiritual insights. They met *themselves*. The highly driven energies required to sustain their daily living were still running on full throttle. But now there were no distractions. There was nothing to 'do'. They felt off balance, empty, anxious and out of control. They wept out of bewilderment and fear. They were meeting the aridity of the frenetic, addictive and consumptive lifestyles that had been driving them for so long they had come to assume it was 'normal'.

Until we just sit down, sit still, we will simply not be aware how distracted our waking lives actually are. And it is only when we enter another way of living we discover how strong are the addictions and compulsions within us. That is what makes sitting down so hard to do.

73

Rumi, the Sunni mystic, is blunt in his advice:

just be quiet and sit down.
… you are drunk,
And this is the edge of the roof. ('The edge of the roof')

There is a monastery I have been visiting for years. I invariably arrive tired, gladly anticipating some 'peace and quiet'. I always go straight to the chapel. In the corner is a simple altar set apart to a special devotion to the presence of Christ in the bread of communion. I kneel. It feels like home. And, most times, I weep with tears of relief. But then for the next 24 hours or so, in that silent house, I know I will be restless, irritable, will pace the gardens without enjoying any of it and binge read in the monastery library. I will make cups of coffee I do not need. I will raid the biscuit tins, keep checking my watch and wait impatiently for the next meal where I will be tempted to eat more than I want. While the tight spring my life has become slowly unwinds I must just sit there. It is the one thing necessary. And as my soul catches up, it is often through the tears that life begins to recover a nurturing flow again.

In strange or hostile places, as in the psalm, where choices and outcomes are uncertain, sitting down is a particular challenge and may take real courage. But it matters because this is the place where, mentally and emotionally, we begin to re-centre. We must be willing just to *be* there, though we may hope for the companionship of others at such times. In the psalm they sat and wept *together*. This is not the moment for analysing anything. In any case we are not reliable judges of what is going on or what we need. Let the fluctuating moods, energies and tears just flow through as they will. All within us is stirred up like a muddy stream. There may be very important stuff there.

But we must let things settle before we can see with any clarity.

In his wonderful book *In the Shelter: finding a Home in the World*, Padraig O Tuama practises the reflex of saying 'hello' to wherever he finds himself and whatever is in front of him. He just greets it all. Hello to here. Hello Babylon. Hello despair. Hello exile. When I tried this I was startled by how it changed my relationship to things around me. Far from being passive acceptance it was a way I began to make relationships with what was given, what is present. And once that happened I could begin to explore my response to this strange place life had brought me to.

Hello to sitting down.

Hello to tears.

19

Remembering

Second reflection on Psalm 137

By the rivers of Babylon ...there we wept when we remembered Zion. (Ps. 137.1)

I have just stood by a war memorial and affirmed, as we do each year, that 'we will remember'. I bought my poppy by a poster that read 'lest we forget'.

But, we might ask, what makes remembering a good thing in a world like this? Aren't many of the most brutal regional conflicts around the world in that state precisely because people can't or won't forget and so are trapped in cycles of revenge and toxic bitterness?

As with an unhealed wound, when something trips against them, the old rift is reopened and violence breaks out.

Memory alone does not save or heal. It may just as easily overwhelm and break us. 'Fifty years and I've never left this place,' wept a survivor on her return to Auschwitz.

I used to visit a man who had been a prisoner in Malaya during the Second World War. He needed no bidding to remember. He was quite unable to forget the violence he saw and endured there. He never spoke of it but the memory was like a shadow across his face at times. During a time of significant fortieth anniversaries in the same war, I was working at a conference centre in North Devon. Regional veteran groups organized reunion trips to the battle sites. One of those who returned was Stan, the maintenance manager at the centre. In the weeks that followed their return from such a trip he and three others in their region took their own lives. Remembering was simply too much to bear.

The costly process of remembering is vividly illustrated in the experience of victims of abuse and torture. The journey towards any kind of healing and new life is often a harrowing one, for they must find a way of recovering their own selves from the depths of the horrors they have endured. This takes immense courage: there were very good reasons for trying to forget. Nor is remembering simply a mental process. Helen Bamber gave her life to working with victims of abuse and torture. She noticed how 'cruelty is above all an experience of the human body'. So an important part of the work of remembering is 'reclaiming "the good body" ... relearning a way of respecting the body *and the self with it*' (Neil Belton, p.135; my italics). The journey of remembering is therefore a physical one. Tears flow at key moments of remembering – whether in anger, pain, relief or fear. They mark moments of connection at the mouth of wounds. Like a river or spring that is being unblocked, tears are a sign that a flow of life is being restored.

One of the Remembrance Day hymns includes the line by Isaac Watts, 'time like an ever-flowing stream ...' But time does not flow smoothly through human history. It clots and coagulates around wounds and hurts. Our personal, family and social histories all have no-go areas, nameless places that are skirted around. We avoid touching on certain issues. Whole communities and nations travel on oblique paths long after the memory of what we are avoiding, and why we are doing so, has faded. We have yet to remember.

The psychotherapist and Holocaust survivor Victor Frankl observed that those who survived concentration camps were not the more powerful, intellectual or clever. They were those who had a sense of inner meaning and therefore of self. In this way it gave them a conviction about who they were and where they were from – something 'to which exploiters do not have access'. This makes sense of the fact that one of the most insistent calls in the Bible is to 'remember'. And this is never more stressed than in times of uncertainty and change. 'Remember me', says God, 'remember Torah', 'remember your story', 'teach your children to remember' (for example: Isa. 46.9; Deut. 24.9; Neh. 1.8; Ps. 42.4, 6).

This work of remembering is not the same as having good memory. It means much more than looking back into the past or recalling dates and events. Memories alone can simply function as justifications for our prejudices. Remembering in this fuller sense is the business of living with the stories and relationships that have made us who we are. In that sense we never leave the past behind. The issue is our relationship with it. To re-member something is to restore our relationship to it. The opposite of remembering in this sense is not forgetting – it is *dis*membering. Re-membering is a work of re-connecting what has been cut off, separated or broken, and bringing it back into a living relationship. But you cannot re-member without first being in touch with what is separated. To begin re-membering we must be present to the wound, to the separation. It must be a work of patient gentleness. The wounds are very tender. What is broken needs holding together tenderly.

At the centre of Christian worship is an act of remembrance. On the night of his betrayal and as his death approached, Jesus hosted a meal for his followers. He broke bread and shared wine and said, 'Do this in remembrance of me' (1 Cor. 11.24).

Disciples of Jesus have shared this in an act of obedience ever since. This is far more than the retelling of a past story. Whether in secret or in public, at a simple kitchen table or on the high altar, in joy or in pain, offered to rich and poor alike, at the beginning of faith or final gift on the lips of the faithful dying, this same meal of bread and wine re-members us.

This is where Christians find hope in our harrowed and forgetful world. What we cannot do for ourselves Christ does for us. In our midst, through suffering, death and resurrection, God, in Christ, re-members us. This is all his work – whatever it takes, at whatever cost.

'There we remembered ...' Remembering is what holds us in being and holds off despair. Everything is at stake here. Though it cannot be the final word, this explains the fierceness and even ferocity with which 'enemies' are identified and resisted in the psalms like this one. Remembering is all. The heart of our identity, belonging and meaning are found here. A future and a hope depend on this.

So there by a strange river, in a hostile land at the far end of exile, they sat down. And with fierce, resistant, defiant tears they remembered Zion.

20

Questioning

Third reflection on Psalm 137

How could we sing the Lord's song
in a foreign land? (Ps. 137.4)

The psalmist has sat down. He has remembered.

On the flow of his tears, heart and mind now turn to the question: 'How am I to live in this place?'

One of the biggest tests of our character is when we find ourselves living where we don't want to be. This is particularly so when we are dependent for our well-being and destiny on the whim or moods of others there. Like the psalmist by the river, we have to work out what choices and responses to make. At the moment he writes, he shows that he can imagine no way his life and faith might have any future. All the familiar landmarks that have given him meaning, security and purpose lie shattered. 'How can I cope, survive, settle, be faithful – or even escape?'

'Questions without answers must be asked very slowly,' wrote Ann Michaels in *Fugitive Pieces* (p.159). The psalmist had no way of knowing how long this journey would last. In fact no one on those forced marches saw their homeland again. It would be another 70 years before the collapse of that empire meant the Jews could return home. The answers the psalmist wanted would only come by waiting. Then, as now, the thought must have felt unbearable.

The remarkably rapid spread of the Christian faith in the first few centuries is too easily assumed to be the outcome of bold, confident faith. We miss just how often the New Testament letters reminded believers to live with 'patience, endurance and perseverance' (for example, Heb. 10.36; Col. 1.11; Rom. 12.12). That suggests a reality that was not for measuring on dramatic graphs of success and growth.

In his research on the dynamics of power in human societies, the sociologist Pierre Bourdieu attached great significance to what he called 'habitus'. This is a quality of character formed by the sheer physical repetition of doing things over and over so that they become habitual and reflexive and shape our embodied existence. The formative power of repetition and rhythm changes things over time. The process seems undramatic, even dull, to modern ears. It is always found in the shadow of the more glossy, confident, strategic plans. Habitus is a quality of presence that is formed through patience and endurance, and Bourdieu insists that its impact over time is what actually transforms whole cultures.

I could wish there was a quicker way of learning patience and endurance! Like many, I do not live well 'between things'. Situations that stay unresolved leave me anxious and irritable. This means I need to take care over the choices I make. I can choose quickly but not wisely, because I simply want to anaesthetize the anxiety by taking action. But in one area of my life I have to live in patience – and so do those who walk with me. I am hearing-impaired. I have lived with this most of my life and generally cope well. But every so often – after a conversation I could not participate in, when over-tired, or after (another) meeting with a poor sound system – it can just boil over. I shed tears of angry frustration. I rage at my powerlessness, at the unfairness, at … – well what words would you add to this list, from your own stories?

Living with chronic, long-term physical disability, Donald Eadie says that a different kind of response is needed. A waiting is required that cannot be tied to time or preferred outcomes: what we most want is not available on those terms so the waiting must remain open-ended. He calls this a 'waiting beyond the waiting'. It means losing control. It asks for a trusting surrender and a willingness to be shaped by 'something that is far beyond our own imaginings' (*A Grain in Winter*, p. 5).

Our culture has no positive use for waiting so we do not come to this insight easily. Everything is focused on doing, on taking action – and doing so ever faster. Waiting is a waste of time. But there is a waiting that is not inactive. Waiting is a poised place of vigilance, curiosity and the willingness to go exploring. On the sports field waiting is the skill that makes the moment to move decisive and game-changing. A waiter in a restaurant is highly alert and ready to respond to need or signal. Faithful waiting is a work of active participation. And this is just how God told his people in Babylon to respond through the prophet Jeremiah: build, plant, marry, multiply - 'seek the welfare of the city where I have sent you into exile, and pray … on its behalf, for in its welfare you will find your welfare' (Jer. 29.5–7).

Donald Winnicott was an internationally renowned, pioneering psychoanalyst. Decades after his death his influence is still immense. What was the secret of his ability to break through the received 'orthodoxies' of his profession to radically new understanding? One of the qualities a colleague noticed in him was his 'monumental ability to contain *un*knowing'. He was a man who could live with questions and was willing to sit in the dark for as long as the answer took to emerge. He could let go of claimed 'certainties' and prevailing ideologies and wait to see where the trail might lead.

It may be that the living that really transforms and changes our world is always 'out of control'. It requires us to let go. As Stanley Hauerwas has written:

> To live out of control is to renounce the illusion that our task as Christians (or simply as human beings) is to make history come out right. Rather, we believe that a more truthful account of what is really going on in the world comes from those who are out of control. For those who are without control have no illusions about what makes this place secure or safe and they inherently distrust those who say they are going to help through power and violence. ('The Servant Community', p. 381)

'And violence is too often the outcome of responses made where patience is absent. The attempt to force an issue, even with good intentions, is a work of coercion. Patience has been wisely defined by Alan Kreider as 'a life that trusts God and therefore does not control things, is not in a hurry and does not use violence' (*The Patient Ferment of the Early Church*, p. 283).

Patience is a quality of life lived in a place of acceptance. After a series of knock backs and rejections in his life, Simon Parke was struggling with anger and resentment. But he tells of coming to another way of responding as he reflected on the difference between resignation and surrender in his situation.

> Resignation is the angry admission that I cannot get my own way; surrender is the peaceful acceptance that 'my own way' cannot be separated from the rest of reality. Resignation is

the attitude of the ego, the separate self, thwarted by reality – and resentfulness. Surrender lets go of such wilfulness, and the idea that the future must conform to my wishes.

All shall be well.

21

Anger

Fourth reflection on Psalm 137

The first verses of Psalm 137 provided the words for one of the best-selling singles of all time in the United Kingdom – 'By the Rivers of Babylon'. But the psalm is also notorious for verses that the song did not include:

> *O daughter Babylon, you devastator!*
> *Happy shall they be who pay you back*
> *what you have done to us!*
> *Happy shall they be who take your little ones*
> *and dash them against the rock! (Ps. 137.8–9)*

This is one of what are called the 'imprecatory psalms' – psalms that unambiguously call for the cursing, judgment and revenge on the enemies of God's people. (Other examples include Pss. 5, 10, 17, 35, 58, 59, 69, 70, 79, 83, 109, 129, 137 and 140.) Though this psalm does not pray to God to act in this way, others do. 'Let them know what you think of them. Blast them with your red-hot anger!' (Ps. 69.24, *The Message*).

'There we wept' - here are tears that lead us deeper into the pain, not away from it.

As the reciting of the psalms has been a traditional part of Christian worship, these vengeful and violent sentiments have always presented a problem. Some modern collections of the psalms place 'offending' verses in brackets so they can be 'safely' omitted – for surely, this implies, they are not 'Christian'? But what is achieved by leaving such feelings unsaid? Feelings do not decompose if you bury them. Am I really free to delete these 'godless' responses from my prayers because by an accident of geography and history I happen to be living in a world where such things do not trouble me?

When the historic Church made the systematic (not selective) reading of the psalms the core of its daily prayer it was saying something important about what praying involves. That a psalm on a particular day may have no relevance to me – anguishing over feelings or experiences that are not part of my life – is not the point. Christian prayer is never just about my personal needs. The psalms are a way we join ourselves to all humanity before God. All of life is there. We stand alongside those whose circumstances are totally different, whose stores may be harrowing beyond description and whose words, out of bitterness or anger, would not be our own. But still we pray *with* their words and longings. And who is to say that if life were treating me as it treats so many others, I would not be saying the same things or worse? In another time and place we may discover the limits of our ability to forgive and a thirst for violent revenge. These prayers are not 'Christian' in what they pray *for*. They are significant for what we confess together before God of our vulnerable humanity and the challenges of living in a violent and uncertain world.

Recent history surely warns us not to underestimate the brutality that those Israelite people would have suffered. For many in the world today have been living through the same kind of horror. For the Israelites of the psalm, the butchering of their children would have been part of the pitiless revenge exacted for their stubborn resistance in the siege of Jerusalem in 597 BCE. Is it really surprising that as the psalmist mourns the dead and remembers the ruins of his homeland and faith, his feelings boil over in raw hatred and a desire for revenge? It is also highly possible that the psalmist and his community are struggling with varying forms of what we now call post-traumatic stress disorder.

The centre of the Christian faith is a place of shocking violence and innocent suffering. Its defining symbol is a cross. In the light of that it is surprising that Christians feel the need to sanitise our language or hide our rawest emotions. Our vocabulary and emotional responses can become too narrow for a world like ours. The cross reveals that God not only takes our worst violence but makes it a means of transforming the world.

My own ministry includes hearing people make their personal confession of sin and ministering to them the forgiveness of Christ. It is a very moving thing to share in. But on a number of occasions, as people have been expressing their sense of guilt out of stories of pain and distress, I have asked them to pause. I suggest to them that they are trying to confess what first needs lamenting and protesting. Before they can own their own failings before God they need to express their anger, rage and lament at whatever has been going on. We easily assume that any kind of anger in us is probably wrong and unchristian. So I urge them to go away, find somewhere private, and pour out their *real* feelings to God with whatever words are needed. These psalms often give them a starting place. When they return to make confession they are always starting from a very different place.

I know a Christian community that was financially defrauded by one of its core members. They took all the appropriate steps required by law. But what remained was what to do with the feeling of anger for the betrayal and deceit by a trusted member of the community. At a meeting of the church council they conducted a final careful review of their responsibilities under church and criminal law. Then they sat in a circle. A cross and a candle were placed on a small table in the middle of the room. They were invited to imagine that the candle represented the presence of Christ in their midst. They were encouraged to talk to him honestly, speaking aloud their thoughts and feelings about this whole painful event. There were tears. There was anger. Some prayed for a particular outcome. Others just said how they were feeling. Some realised they were not ready to forgive. It took courage. They had never spoken or prayed together in such a way before. The pain would need time to heal. Seeking love and reconciliation from the wounds of betrayal does not come quickly or easily. But the honesty of bringing those feeling into the open – and offering them to the cross of Christ – was very important.

There are many artistic expressions of the cross. But there is one I find particularly helpful, the Verney Cross (see p. 89). Instead of an empty cross or the figure of Jesus fastened on to two wooden beams it comprises two painfully jagged, separated pieces. The figure of Jesus is the space between the two pieces. In his own body he holds them together – a space that is his suffering presence. His arms are thrust into the midst of the broken pieces. When I pray it is into that space that I offer the world and its needs. At times I lay this cross flat and imagine the space as a pool where the tears of the world mingle with the tears of Christ's own suffering. It is deep and wide enough for it all.

All of life is there.

The Verney Cross. This is a sketch of a cross being designed by Scilla Verney. She was dying of cancer at the time, so, perhaps appropriately, it is unfinished. I am grateful to her late husband for permission to use it.

22

Grief

Jesus began to weep. (John 11.35)

Jesus had just arrived at the tomb of his close friend, Lazarus. At the sight of Mary and Martha, Lazarus' sisters, weeping with their friends, his own tears began flowing. That is not unusual. The tears of others can easily trigger our own. Those watching him assumed he was grieving for his friend. 'See how he loved him' (John 11.36). And indeed the love Jesus had for Lazarus and his sisters is stressed throughout this story. Their home, a few miles outside Jerusalem, was a special refuge for Jesus.

The ministry of Jesus can be summed up by the word 'compassion'. The word expresses

> such a deep and central emotion in Jesus that it can only be described as a movement of the womb of God. When Jesus was moved to compassion, the source of all life trembled, the ground of love burst open, and the abyss of God's immense, inexhaustible and unfathomable tenderness revealed itself. (Donald McNeill, Douglas Morrison, Henri Nouwen, pp. 16-17).

There by the tomb, in the midst of grieving loved ones, the tears of divine compassion are dramatically revealed. The words used express both deep grief and anger. 'He shuddered, moved with the deepest emotions' as Raymond Brown's translation puts it (p. 321). Tears and anger, vulnerability and strength come together here in a way we do not always expect.

Jesus missed both the death and funeral of Lazarus. He is sharply questioned for this by Martha and the reason for his delayed arrival unfolds in the dramatic story that follows. But in his absence at such a moment Jesus has much in common with many in Western society today. Increasingly people in our culture are not present at the dying or the funeral of loved ones; something previous generations would have found very shocking. Social and religious customs around the way we observe death have been changing fast. One example of this is the growing number of church funerals I have attended in recent years where the body of the deceased is not present. A private service at the crematorium has happened earlier in the day or even the day before. The service to which friends and community are invited is called a 'Thanksgiving for the life of ...' . The mood is positive and celebratory. It is not uncommon to be told to wear bright clothing.

This means that the community (and sometimes even the family) no longer gives time and place for the important work of saying goodbye and of committal. Increasingly the body is not treated as relevant or necessary for this. Crematorium chapel design often contributes to it. The coffin is often on a catafalque on one side, with the minister's stall on the other. There may be no contact or focus on the coffin. It may as well not be there. A remote button triggers the curtains closing around the coffin and it is simply left there while mourners leave by a door on the other side of the chapel. Many of the choices made for the content and actions in one of these services tend to be concerned primarily with avoiding upsetting the mourners.

There is a growing enthusiasm for something called 'direct

cremations'. The name means what it implies. The coffin is taken direct from the place of death straight to the crematorium. There is no service. Friends or loved ones are not present. David Bowie is one who has given publicity to this way of death. As Rosie Millard puts it, 'people are starting to opt out of their own funerals'.

The striking thing about the websites offering this is how impersonal their language is. There is brief mention of 'your loved one' in the opening sentences, but all the emphasis that follows is on saving money: 'You can have a loved one cremated for less than £1,000'; and also of the convenience of not having to make any of the traditional arrangements: 'There is no viewing, visitation, or wake before the cremation, which eliminates the need for embalming or other body preparations' (see the Everplans website). But it eliminates a lot else, including important ways we need to be present and to grieve. It eliminates saying goodbye. It eliminates the bodies of those whose life we have known and shared in flesh and blood – and whose remains now need a reverent returning to the earth, whether as body or ashes.

By contrast, I attended the funeral of a friend. His coffin was central to the service and was treated with a holy reverence. Two friends circled slowly round it 'censing' it with incense with tender care, swinging the incense burner over every part and into every corner and join. Inside was a cancer-wasted body, but it was being treated with infinite honour. Grief and gratitude mingled together. Loss and hope combined. In Christian faith life comes *through* death, not in attempts at by-passing it.

The emotional constraints within much British culture mean that even funerals have become places where grief is repressed. I have too often heard the bereaved at a graveside or in the crematorium garden being congratulated for being 'strong'. That means they were not crying. What kind of strength is appropriate or commendable alongside the lifeless body of a loved one?

Kate Bowler is a theology professor and a mother with a young family. She also has stage four cancer. She describes grief as 'eyes squinting through tears into an unbearable future'. Her article about her journey with cancer created a huge impact when it was published in *The New York Times*. But it was the response from within her own faith communities she found hardest. 'I think churches in general are horrible at being sad,' she says. 'My point [in *The New York Times*] was, "Please don't force certainty on my pain," and then, one minute later, people poured certainty on my pain. Everyone is trying to Easter the crap out of my Lent!' ('Wishing Job's Comforter's Well').

Grief unexpressed comes at a price. Pastoral experience suggests that unshed tears do not simply go away. 'Feelings do not decompose if you bury them,' the saying goes. Suppressed, they will find expression in less helpful ways. Susanna Tamarro expresses it very vividly: 'Unshed tears leave a deposit on your heart. Eventually they form a crust around it and paralyze it, the way mineral deposits paralyze a washing machine.'

The Sky sports presenter Simon Thomas has written movingly of the death of his wife just days after she was diagnosed with leukaemia. He reflects on what it means to be strong in a place of overwhelming loss, quoting some words he found on a blog site. 'When life is tough they tell you to be strong. Don't be strong. Be weak. Unclench your fists. Dare to be vulnerable. Honest weakness takes courage. It affirms our common humanity, deepens friendship and elicits grace.' Simon Thomas continues:

> All I can do at the moment is unclench those fists, stop trying to be strong and just say to people this is me. This is what grief feels like. This is what it feels like when the person you loved

so deeply suddenly disappears from your life. This is what it feels like when your hopes, dreams and plans as a family get ripped apart and shredded. This is what vulnerability looks like, and right now I can't be any other way, and as I've now discovered, this is what being strong actually looks like.

Can we imagine Jesus arriving in the midst of the griefs in our lives and elsewhere in our world today? He is late again, as he was then, in a sense that Martha challenged him with, 'If you had been here, my brother would not have died' (John 11.21). But the effect of coming late was to reveal his presence in a new way. Jesus wept. He is moved from his depths with heart-broken, indignant tears, for death is the ultimate affront to a God who is a life-giver.

Those deep, shuddering tears are what God's strength actually looks like.

23

The bread of tears

You have fed them with the bread of tears, and made them drink a triple measure of tears. (Ps. 80.6; Robert Alter, *The Book of Psalms*, p. 285).

This is a very strong statement, even an accusation. It is addressed to God.

Psalm 80 is thought to have originated when the threat of the great Assyrian army was looming like a menacing shadow on Israel's northern border. But they had clearly been feeling neglected and exposed for some time. The psalmist reminds God he saved his people out of Egypt and planted them here in the land, behind secure walls like a well-protected vineyard. So why, asks the psalmist, have you now broken down those walls 'so that all who pass along the way pluck its fruit?' (Ps. 80.12). 'Restore', 'save', 'shine' are words that repeat like a refrain through the psalm. This crisis needs God's light and salvation. And four times God is addressed as the 'Lord, God of Armies' (v. 4, Alter). But the one who should be organizing his forces against their enemies has breached his own people's defences, leaving them undefended and at the mercy of any who are passing.

It is startling behaviour God is being accused of. But though he is angry with them, God has not deserted his people. He is still providing for them: but it is the bread of tears. What kind of God feeds his people on tears? What kind of nourishment is only available through such grief?

Trace the history of God's people through the Bible and you see that one of the lessons they have to learn again and again is not to treat God as a kind of personal chaplain – there to bless *them*, provide for *their* needs, favour *their* interests and make *them* important in the world. It is a familiar temptation for nations throughout history, particularly in times of wealth and power, to claim themselves to be the object of God's special love and favour. Of course this is dressed up in devout, religious language and behaviour. Church services may be full, and it can all look very pious. But God is not fooled. This is an attempt at consumer religion, a faith of self-interest.

God loves – but he loves *wisely*. Not all tears are for comforting immediately, like an indulgent parent who comes running at every cry, offering immediate comforts and distractions. Nor are tears a measure of sincerity or honesty. We may just be hurting. The question here is whether those tearful pleas are expressing an actual change of heart. Is this the prayer of those who are ready to mend their ways? The psalm contains all sorts of promises to God: save us and 'we will never turn back from you' (Ps. 80.18). But is this faith or bargaining? Do we even know ourselves?

God does a tough but loving thing in such circumstances. He simply withdraws his protection. He refuses to be *useful*. God's people are exposed to their full vulnerability and need. They are forced to face the presumptions of their theology and behaviour. They are humbled by their fears. And, perhaps, they return to the Lord.

In this sense the psalm may be expressing an awakening. Although God is still being called upon to take action, the fact that this prayer is being prayed at all is significant. A people going through desolation and facing abandonment and defeat are crying out. They know who they must turn to. Then, as now, the greatest crisis in any age is always God.

The first Sunday of the Christian year is called Advent. The name comes from the Latin *venio* – meaning 'come'. And that is the focus – the coming of God. But it means more than that. If *venio* means come, *ad-venio* means I come *against*. It is the season where we come up against God. And Psalm 80 is one of the psalms read during this season.

When I can, I attend a cathedral service of lessons and carols by candle-light on this day. One moment always moves me. It is not a reading or carol. It is a long silence. At the start of the service all the lights are turned out. In that packed cathedral we sit in the dark for an extended time holding candles we have no means to kindle. This acts out something profound at the heart of faith. We are seeking something only God can give. We cannot make anything happen. Nor can we demand it. It can only be a gift. We wait in the dark for the light to come.

In an unexpected and perhaps prophetic sermon at the consecration of a bishop, the preacher, Stephen Cottrell, spoke of the painful but essential experience of darkness in the life of faith. It cannot be all light and blessing. Like the gift of the bread of tears, this too is God's work. There is no other way. There will be times when

we have to let God lead us to a place of darkness, unknowing. And there, in the utter lostness of that place, he will turn us around, and show us his way ... there have been, and will be, moments of wretchedness and darkness, when I don't know what I'm doing and I don't know what to say. And in these moments, like in the gospel itself, where the sky blackens as Jesus hangs upon the cross, and where God raises him in the darkness before the dawn, it is in the refining emptiness of these moments that I learn to trust God and become again his voice and his hands to do his will and purpose for the world.

Then addressing the gathered congregation he said:

Let him take all the rich experiences of [your] lives and ministry and let him cleanse and refine you. Be 'an instrument in God's hands' so that Christ may be known. Let him lead you into the darkness as well as into light.

Elaine Heath goes even further. The church today will not grow and flourish again simply because it gets its methods right, she writes. It must not presume upon God's blessing even for strategies launched in his name. Rather,

> a dark night is descending on the church … a divinely initiated process of loss so that the accretion of the world, the flesh and the devil may be recognised and released … a process of purgation and de-selfing … it holds the possibilities of new beginnings. Liberation takes place in hidden ways, beneath our knowledge and understanding. The church will persevere not because of church programs, but because God's love has kept it. (*The Mystic Way of Evangelism*, pp. 27-29)

This is the gift of a God who loves enough to feed his people with the sharp nourishment of grief. The bread of tears is found here.

24

The valley of Baca

One of my favourite psalms in the Bible is a song of joyful anticipation. 'My soul has a desire and longing to enter the courts of the Lord' (Ps. 84.1–2, *Common Worship*). It was sung by pilgrims on their way to worship in the Temple in Jerusalem. But a brief verse in it refers to a particular part of the journey.

> *As they [the pilgrims] go through the valley of Baca*
> *they make it a place of springs.* (Ps. 84.6)

That valley seems to have had a reputation. It is sometimes translated as the 'valley of dryness', though the reference is to the season rather than the terrain. The reference to Baca (Balsam) trees suggests another association. 'Balsam' also sounds like the Hebrew word for 'tears'. For this reason, early Bible versions called it the 'vale of tears' and it became a familiar expression for earthly life as a whole.

The valley of Baca is a metaphor for those occasions that come to us all at different times, when life becomes a dried-out, weary struggle. They are places without refreshment or comfort, where we face discouragement, disappointment and exhaustion. No discussion of tears is complete without acknowledging these valleys.

A society that runs on such high levels of emotional stimulation as ours requires the managing of periods of emotional exhaustion. An increasing amount of attention is being given to something called 'compassion fatigue'. Organizations involved in providing care for others are paying increasing attention to the emotional welfare of their staff.

> Caring too much can hurt. When caregivers focus on others without practicing self-care, destructive behaviors can surface. Apathy, isolation, bottled up emotions and substance abuse head a long list of symptoms associated with the secondary traumatic stress disorder now labeled: Compassion Fatigue. (Compassion Fatigue Awareness Project)

We are also a society in which people are living longer while practical and financial provision for the health and welfare of the elderly and disabled are being progressively cut back. Around one in ten people are giving regular unpaid care to relatives or friends. This burden can be considerable. Some have no choice but to put their own lives and needs on hold in order to fulfil the task of caring that has fallen to them. It can be very difficult to find the personal resources they need to sustain their own well-being.

Compassion fatigue is not dramatic in its onset so it is possible not even to be aware of its presence. For some years part of my work was to guide Christian ministers planning periods of sabbatical leave. I would begin by asking them what they were hoping for out of such a time. All too often, the only thing they knew was that they needed a rest. The task was to work through layers of exhaustion until they re-engaged with the sources of life and inspiration that first drew them into this work and to which they had given themselves so long and sacrificially. Not all could.

Charities speak of 'donor fatigue'. The range of people's needs is endless. Media coverage brings us into close contact with suffering in harrowing detail, and often without warning. This intensity both motivates and exhausts us. I confess there are times I can hardly bring myself to read the newspaper or watch the television news. It is just too overwhelming. But then I feel guilty and ashamed. How can I switch off from what others are going through? I surely lack compassion?

There are certainly times when the challenge is to care more and to renounce indifference and self-interest. But we are reflecting here on the cost of sustaining our commitment and compassion.

If our involvement in a needy world is simply driven by the restless interests of the media, our responses will always tend to be reactive. That adds to our stress. An example is the divisive issue of immigration, which has returned to the political debate. For a while the levels of hostility were high, fuelled by press stories of migrants taking people's jobs and houses or exploiting the benefits system. Sympathy for the thousands of desperate people risking their lives trying to cross the Mediterranean on flimsy overcrowded boats was in consequence at a low ebb.

Then a photograph appeared on the front page of a newspaper. A little boy was lying face down on a Greek shoreline. He had drowned when his boat had capsized. Suddenly the horrors of another world become unavoidably real. As the human angle of the crisis came to the fore the emotional shock was huge. Newspapers that had been campaigning against immigration were now shrill with moral indignation. Politicians were criticized for their inaction. Donations to charities peaked – for a short time.

Symptoms of compassion fatigue include:

- Emotional exhaustion – sometimes called 'emotional blunting' or numbing. This can be confused with lack of compassion.
- A reduced sense of personal accomplishment or meaning in work.
- Mental exhaustion resulting in loss of concentration levels.
- Decreased interaction with others and therefore a growing isolation.
- Physical exhaustion.

What is required are forms of emotional self-management. These include:

- Seeking out people to talk to.
- Taking exercise and eating properly.
- Taking some time off and getting enough sleep.
- Developing interests outside of the immediate situation.
- Identifying what is important to *you* and seeking to give space for it.

Responses to guard against include:

- Restlessly looking for a new job, buying a new car, getting a divorce or having an affair.
- Falling into the habit of complaining.
- Working harder and longer.
- Relying on self-medication.
- Neglecting your own needs and interests (see Compassion Fatigue Awareness Project).

Much of this advice applies to sustaining spiritual life as well. The New Testament adds a further piece of wisdom. Those vulnerable first Christian communities were urged to 'hold fast to what is good' (1 Thess. 5.21). Bad news can suck all hope out of us. One way of focusing on the positive is to be committed to specific causes. We simply cannot love and care for everything, everywhere. We need commitments *some*where. This may be a particular charity or community. We stay with their work whether it is in the news or not, supporting them in their struggles, celebrating the good times and 'success' stories, however fragile.

In ordination services of the Church of England candidates are warned that the task before them is too great to undertake in their own strength. They are urged to pray, 'that your hearts would daily be enlarged'. This is a metaphor for the wide generosity we need in order to love and care in a world like ours. In the poetry of the psalm, sustaining the journey through that valley involves looking for the springs, those hidden sources of life flowing below the barren surface. The psalm is confident they are there: 'they make it a place of springs' (Ps. 84.6). Our search too is for the inner resources that sustain us to the journey's end. Our hope too is that we, like those ancient pilgrims:

- become springs of healing for others
- reservoirs of compassion to those who are bruised
- God will be there at the end of their journey (Ps.84.7, Jim Cotter, p. 73).

25

Fire and water

Our society has been described as living on the 'compass of our excitement'. We are driven at high levels of emotional intensity that leave us restless, reactive and impulsive. We go wherever the needle points next. We get bored and tire quickly. Attention spans are short. Strength of feeling is the measure of what is most important. The quality most valued is to be 'passionate'. It doesn't even really matter what you are passionate about. It could be world poverty, gardening or coffee.

The journalist Deborah Orr writes with concern for a society where people have so little understanding of their emotions or control over them that

> they sooner or later coagulate into a roiling soup of anxiety, fear, sadness, self-loathing, resentment and anger, which expresses itself however it can, finding objects to project its hurt and confusion on to. Like immigrants. Or transsexuals. Or liberals. Or Tories. Or women. Or men.

But we are much more than a stormy mix of passions and feelings. We are creatures of desire. The journey we need, says Philip Sheldrake, is 'from a multitude of desires, or from surface desires, to our deepest desires which, as it were, contains all that is true and vital about ourselves' (*Befriending Your Desires*, p. 16). In the monastic world, at the moment of making vows of commitment, an important question is asked: 'What is your desire?' Much careful prayer and extended reflection has led up to this moment. But at that point of consecration of life and calling the discerning of desire is central.

If that question were asked of you at this stage in your life and story, do you know how you would reply? In my experience people find that a hard question to answer. In fact we often have a stronger sense of what we do *not* desire – a frustration with the life we have been living and a persistent sense of something missing. But we struggle to find the language with which to talk about and name our deeper desires. And even if we think we know 'what I really want', can we be sure it is true? Do we really know ourselves at all?

Someone was telling me of their frustrations with their present job. They had not been in it long and it was not what they had hoped it would be. As we talked it became clear this was the latest in a series of such disappointments. Life kept letting him down. He was angry and frustrated. It was easy to pin the blame on others for the situation – the organisation, the Church, a particular manager. The problem was always somewhere, or with some*one*, else. But there was something almost addictive in the way his personal choices repeatedly put him back into those situations. Where such patterns emerge, something deeper is going on. What is not changed is being *chosen*. Those moments where our choices have let us down (again!) are places we can stop and begin to test our desires more carefully.

To desire and to feel intensely are not the same thing. I am quite capable of feeling very passionate about something only for my interest to drift off after a while. Nor is strength of emotion a measure of the depth of significance – still less of wisdom or maturity. Unless we face this, our appetites can lead us terribly astray. As Gregory of Nyssa said:

A person can spin a whole net of falsities around their spirit by the repeated consecration of the whole self to values that do not exist. They exhaust themselves in the pursuit of mirages that ever fade, and are renewed as fast as they have faded, drawing them further and further into the wilderness where they must die of thirst. (Margaret Magdalene, p. 24)

We must learn to desire. As we continue to discover, the place where tears surface is a good starting place.

If our lives are running on such high levels of emotional overstimulation tears may, in the first instance, be offering a necessary release of tension – like a squall of rain passing through, the tears drench everything and then move on. At other times tears will be a genuine cry for help and comfort and a plea to be treated gently. Tears can be speaking the language of despair and the terror of feeling overwhelmed. Tears may flow from frustration and helplessness with life or from joy in moments of life fulfilled.

But tears can also be an attempt at control. For example, if a conversation gets too challenging, tears are a very effective way of deflecting questions that are too disturbing to face. In my experience churches and volunteer organisations, perhaps with their focus on caring, can be easier targets for what we might call 'tactical tears'. The person weeping would of course protest at the idea their tears were a means of power and control at such times.

I have known meetings brought to a halt because someone became 'upset' at a certain point in the discussion. Not only was the person too distressed for the meeting to continue, others in the room became upset because that person was upset! The result was emotional paralysis. In one such instance I knew that the tears were nothing to do with the decision in hand. Rather, they revealed a person with a deep fear of taking responsibility – almost certainly based on the unfaced pain of an earlier life experience.

On one occasion, sharing a difficult personal decision that I knew would hurt others, I wept as I spoke to them. I thought my tears were showing them how much I cared and that this hurt me too. Only under the firm probing of a wise friend did I subsequently see how thoroughly manipulative I had been. My tears effectively blocked my friends from speaking to me, or even challenging me, as they needed to.

Passion and desire are more often linked to fire than water. We burn with longing. We are aflame with desire. Fire is the spiritual language of purifying and forging. It consumes what is dross and reveals what is enduring. But the ancient spiritual writers regularly spoke of water and fire together. Without any sense of contradiction an ancient Eastern liturgy speaks of God 'recasting our image in baptism as in a furnace', and making 'his own handiwork in the furnace of water and the heat of the Spirit'. The metaphors keep interweaving. 'Tears flow from your eyes like fountains of water [as the heart] is kindled with the power of the Spirit within you as with fire' (Maggie Ross, p. 234). The water and the fire are one in the purifying and restoring work of God in our lives. And our most passion-filled hope is this – that 'at the heart of all of us is a centre that is a point of intersection where my deepest desire and God's desiring in me meet and are found to coincide' (Philip Sheldrake, p. 17).

26

Till we have faces

I was listening to someone as he talked about a particular aspect of his life. He was interesting, though quite self-contained and firmly in control of the story. At a certain point tears began to accompany his words. He was a stranger to his tears and was quite thrown by them, suddenly awkward and losing all fluency in his narrative. But for just a fleeting moment a different face appeared through the tears – like a flicker across his countenance.

Tears flow from the most authentic places within us. So they both reveal and betray us – to ourselves as well as to others.

I lived for some years in a residential Christian community. Most of the community were young men and women on a gap year or two helping to run a large conference and holiday centre. It was a very exciting place to be and most of us arrived with a high idealism about what shared Christian living would be like. There was a sense that 'if we can't make it work here where can it work?' Well, by the grace of God it did 'work', but not in the ways we had planned. All joining the community had a probation period for growing into the shared life and work of the place. Full community promises were not made until three months had passed. There was wisdom in this. Three months proved to be the length of time it took most of us simply to run out of steam! We each, in our own way, had to reach the point where we knew we could not make this work by our own efforts. Often that moment of realisation was triggered by a crisis – a falling out with a community member or guest. It was always a shock to discover we had no love left even to be polite, still less perfect.

One of the promises made at the moment of full commitment was: 'Are you open to being known for who you are?' It was the *willingness* that was being asked of us at this point. That was the only 'yes' needed. There was no assumption we knew who we were at all, which was just as well. We all came into community from quite mixed and often fractured stories of belonging and relationships. For many it was the first experience of sustained love and acceptance, so it was as vulnerable as it was exciting. All our well-practised tactics for being liked, for gaining approval, our well-polished public images, had to go – usually through sheer exhaustion. They were simply not sustainable for long in the demands of shared life and ministry. It is always frightening to come to that place of powerlessness. And it always feels like failure. Not surprisingly this was the place of many tears. Tears are often a sign of a loss or surrender of power and control. But in the Christian journey they are also a sign of entering something new. Jesus often said that to find your life you must lose it (Matt. 10.39).

What I remember is how people's faces often changed over this time – or, rather, began to emerge. Tears were central to this. Old, hardened defences and self-chosen 'images' steadily dissolved away. Life's scars and wounds were bathed. Faces sometimes aged but gained in sensitivity, beauty and depth. Eyes often became clearer. It was a journey of vulnerability, much hesitancy and often requiring immense courage. But it was very moving to watch an authentic 'self' emerging – becoming more alive, less needing to defend, more free to live and even to play. We cared less but loved more.

Some years ago a psychologist called Philip Cushman

published an influential paper called *Why the Self is Empty*. His starting point was that our sense of self – that secure sense of who we are in the world – was profoundly under threat. Our 'self' is not something we are born with. It is something we develop as we grow in the community of shared life. Traditionally home and family were supported in this process by various social organisations and institutions that also enshrined the life and values of a culture and passed them on to the next generation – typically these included uniformed organisations, church, sport and social clubs, unions and political parties. But nearly all these community institutions and networks of relationships are collapsing. They can no longer offer secure places of belonging and attachment. The result is that the self is empty. We have no way of knowing ourselves. Emotionally and psychologically we experience this as a deep, indiscriminate hunger. Cushman notes the prevalence of addictive and consumptive disorders in today's world. Consumer society started as an emotional hunger before it became an economic strategy.

This explains in part our obsession with celebrity and media image. We are looking for an image and likeness through which to begin to know our selves. But which image do we trust? We are never more vulnerable than in this search. Our very selves are at stake. A feature of social media that so dominates human interaction today is how image-focused it is. And it is not surprising to find research revealing its damaging effect on the mental and emotional health of young people. Recent surveys of Snapchat and Facebook show worrying levels of anxiety, negative body image, low self-esteem and the fear of missing out. This in turn leaves young people vulnerable to manipulation and on-line bullying (see Dennis Campbell's article in *The Guardian*, 'Facebook and Twitter Harm Young People's Mental Health').

We live with a dilemma: we no longer know who we are or

what we look like. And we cannot be sure who we can trust to tell us.

Christianity is a religion of faces. The unseen God reveals his own image to us in the face of Christ (2 Cor. 4.6). But in taking human form Christ meets us in our *own* image and likeness. There is a mutual turning – face to face. Jesus gives us back to ourselves.

In a beautiful reflection, C. S. Lewis anticipates the time when we finally see the face of God. It will be like one of those times when we pass someone in the street or see them across a crowded room and think, 'I'm *sure* I know that face.'

> When we see the face of God we shall know that we have always known it. He has been a party to, has made, sustained and moved moment by moment within, all our earthly experiences of innocent love. All that was true love in them was, even on earth, far more His than ours, and ours only because His. (*The Four Loves*, p. 137)

27

Encountering mercy

Lament and mourn and weep. Let your laughter be turned into mourning and your joy into dejection. (James 4.9)

For some a verse like this confirms their worst suspicions about the Bible and religious faith – joy-denying, self-hating and sin-obsessed. The Greek word for mourning does not easily translate into English. *Penthos* is not simply feeling miserable or wretched about ourselves. It has a very particular focus. *Penthos* expresses a Godly grief, a holy mourning and longing that comes from a heart broken with an awareness of its deepest need.

We have to pray for *penthos*. It does not come naturally to us. It can only be given. Spiritual guides urge us to yearn and long for it. *Penthos* comes through the gift of 'compunction'. We probably understand this word better in its negative form. To act *without* compunction is to behave without pity, sensitivity, conscience or any capacity for recognising our wrong. Compunction, by contrast, is an awakening to new awareness. It means 'the sharp prick of conscience'. 'Puncture' comes from the same root. Compunction is the action of the Holy Spirit, puncturing our falsely inflated, self-deceiving views of ourselves, deflating us to an awareness of how deeply we are cut off from our true life in God. It is painful but healing. A severe mercy.

The hardened heart, or heart of stone, is another way the

Bible often speaks of the unconverted life (Ezek. 36.26). For the gift of tears in compunction the spiritual writers make poetic use of the story from the wilderness where God's people are complaining, faithless and without water. Moses is told to strike the rock in the wilderness. It breaks open and water gushes out (Num. 20.2–8).

It is not surprising that tears were often seen as the surest sign that this sorrow was genuine, sincere and a work of the Spirit. But as we noted in Chapter 4, not all people weep. So whenever tears are discussed in this context a pastoral awareness can be found towards those whose eyes are dry but whose hearts are no less open to God.

Christian worship usually includes prayers for confession of sin. Bible readings and preaching routinely stress sin too. But I had been a Christian for a long time before confession became a reality. I knew of the ancient ministry of sacramental confession (the practice of going to confess formally before a priest and receiving forgiveness) but I had never done it. Some churches tended to look on the practice with suspicion. I knew my need of help with areas of conscience and action where I was making no headway and felt guilty. There was no break with sin or relief of heart. So I arranged to meet with a priest I respected and in the side chapel of a church, with the list I had prepared, I knelt in front of a severe crucifix and confessed my sins to God. I began to weep. I felt ashamed as I never had before.

When I had finished the priest took my list from me and tore it up. It was no longer mine, he said. Christ had dealt with it. He laid hands on my head and declared that in the name of Christ I was forgiven and uncondemned. He then prayed for my blessing and a renewed gift of the Spirit. My tears continued but now expressed relief and joy. I felt that a weight was lifted off me. I was also aware of a fresh resolve to turn to new ways of living and believing. I understood what Richard Foster calls the 'liberating shock of repentance'.

I continued to go to confession a few times a year as part of my spiritual discipline. It was not always accompanied by tears but there was always a sense of burden lifted and gift received. The priest would sometimes offer counsel. More often he gave me a penance. A penance is the spiritual equivalent of physiotherapy – exercises for heart, mind and will to build up muscle that has been lacking strength for the task. This usually took the form of a hymn to sing that celebrated the aspect of God and faith I most needed to be focusing on.

'Grant us *true* repentance' is the wise ancient prayer. Not all tears are sincere. Not all grief leads to change of heart. It can look very pious and holy but it may be only that – for show. I may be confessing my guilt in a bid to preserve some self-respect in the midst of humiliation and shame – playing the 'pious penitent' but not wanting to change my life at all. As Jean Pierre de Caussade wrote, 'There is a kind of dramatic sorrow for sin which is actually nothing but pride; the truest contrition is the least conscious of itself'. And there is a saying, 'Many confess, but few repent!'

There is true and false repentance. One of the clearest distinctions between the two is the way false repentance leaves a person preoccupied with themselves. True repentance leads to self-*forgetting* and joyful freedom.

The comedian Russell Brand has written of his struggles with severe chemical and behavioural addictions. His recovery has been through the familiar 12-step programme which begins with the confession that we are powerless to change ourselves. To the surprise of his followers the journey has led him to an awakened interest in the Christian faith. 'My personal feeling is the teachings of Christ are more relevant now than they've ever been.' He tells of how 'my route to spirituality comes through addiction, so it comes from defeat, destruction, annihilation of self in a very humiliating way, I suppose. I had no choice but to embrace spiritual life, but now I am grateful for this. It makes sense of my life'. That rock-bottom moment is the severe gift of compunction that leads to true *penthos*.

Only the sinner understands the gospel, for only the sinner knows their need of it.

In the holy gift of *penthos* there is a strong link between tears and joy. The connection is often made in the psalms:

Weeping may linger for the night,
*   but joy comes with the morning. (Ps. 30.5)*

May those who sow in tears
*   reap with shouts of joy.*
Those who go out weeping,
*   bearing the seed for sowing,*
shall come home with shouts of joy,
*   carrying their sheaves. (Ps. 126.5–6)*

One of the marks of 'sinners' who encounter the mercy and love of Jesus in the Gospels is their joy. A friend remembers the enormous, sustained impact of her encounter with God's love and mercy when she became a Christian as an adult out of quite a troubled life. 'When I was "saved", I cried for months, every time I thought of something awful I had done. The tears continued in gratitude and awe at God's forgiveness. It was a kind of extended repentance. It was very cathartic.'

'Blessed are those who have *penthos*,' said Jesus - only they know the joy of being wrong.

28

Lament

There is a particular way of expressing pain in the Bible, largely absent from the Church and the culture of the Western world. It is called *lament*. Over two-thirds of the psalms start there, with questioning, grief and protest: 'Answer me when I call, O God!' (Ps. 4.1); 'Why, O Lord do you stand far off?' (Ps. 10.1); 'Rise up, O Lord...do not forget the oppressed' (Ps. 10.12); 'Attend to me, and answer me; I am troubled in my complaint' (Ps. 55.2).

Jeremiah was often called 'the Weeping Prophet'. He felt the distress of his people so deeply he could 'hear' their tears.

> *A voice is heard in Ramah,**
> *lamentation and bitter weeping.*
> *Rachel is weeping for her children;*
> *she refuses to be comforted for her children,*
> *because they are no more* (Jer. 31.15)

(*Ramah was a city in ancient Israel, somewhere north of Jerusalem. The name means 'height' and it was particularly exposed on the main invasion route for armies from the north. It suffered much slaughter and Rachel, an ancient mother figure in Israel, is figuratively described here as mourning for her dead offspring.)

Jeremiah's anguish was so overwhelming at times that he prayed for a greater capacity to weep.

O that my head were a spring of water,
and my eyes a fountain of tears,
so that I might weep day and night
for the slain of my poor people! (Jer. 9.1)

By contrast, the theological teacher Walter Brueggemann notes the way that 'the church has by and large, continued to sing songs of orientation [i.e. of confident security and stability] in a world increasingly experienced as *dis*orientated' (*The Message of the Psalms*, p. 51). Politicians and organizations do the same. This could be brave defiance. More probable is that in these disturbing times we lack, or are avoiding, the language we need to express what is going on and our responses to it.

But the pain of the world needs somewhere to go. It does not decompose if we simply bury it. We need a spirituality that helps us face and express this. As the poet Ovid said, 'Suppressed grief suffocates.' This is the work of lament.

'Lamentations' is possibly the most neglected book in the Bible. It is an extended, raw lament over the destruction of Jerusalem and the holy Temple. This book is rarely read or preached on in church. But there are millions today who would recognise only too well the harrowed world described in its pages. It has been suggested there are three reasons why this is an important book for the contemporary world. First, to avoid lament is to disrespect and exclude the voices of those who are in the midst of overwhelming suffering and pain. Lamentations is a call to remember and identify with them (see Chapter 19). Second, without it we are deprived of a language with which to pray in and for what is happening. Finally, if we exclude lament we avoid the challenge of wrestling with faith and God where we need it most. The question 'why' does not go away.

Reflecting on the relationship of the prophets to God in

difficult times, the Jewish philosopher Abraham Heschel stresses the importance of protest and argument.

> The refusal to accept the harshness of God's ways in the name of his love was an authentic form of prayer. [A person] who lived by honesty could not be expected to suppress anxiety when tormented by profound perplexity. They had to speak out audaciously... There are some forms of suffering we must accept with love and bear in silence. There are other items to which we must say no! (Henri Nouwen, *The Genesee Diary*, p.142).

But he goes on to note how this anger is not only the complaint of a suffering people *against* God. It contains a loving concern for God's own name and honour in the world. Lament includes compassion *for* God.

Jesus pronounces a specific blessing upon those who mourn (Matt. 5.4). He is not saying that grief is good. This is about the capacity to live near to it, not avoiding or denying the 'negative' emotion that accompanies it. We are to name it and feel it deeply. There is an African saying: 'Make room for sister grief by the fire.' It must have its place. And when it does, Jesus promises it will be comforted. The Rwandan church is still living with terrible memories of genocide and slaughter. The services include celebration and dance. But there is always a moment where the mourners make their entrance too. All Christian worship needs to give space and voice to those who cannot celebrate. We are called to 'weep with those who weep' – not cheer them up! (Rom. 12.15).

Lament is a very particular response of faith in the presence of human pain and perplexity. It is not the same as grumbling or moaning, which is essentially immature. The Bible knows the difference. Christopher Wright described it as 'the furnace of dire experience in this fallen world' and 'a house for sorrow and a school for compassion' (*The Book of Lamentations*, p. 23). Grumblers rarely turn up for that and are usually nameless. Lament is a way of being active, faithful and responsible in the midst of what is happening.

Little in my Christian pilgrimage taught me about the prayer of lament. Christian living was spoken of more in terms of submission. But those places of anger and protest in the Bible reveal a closeness to God – not a distance. It takes faith and love to be angry like that. You would not bother otherwise. The words and tears of lament are first of all an insistence on being present to what is going on, in the grief and pain. But lament includes a protest and refusal to tolerate or submit to what is going on in the name of humanity or God.

The meeting was long and unproductive. I now realise it was adding to a deepening anguish within I had not found a way of expressing. On the surface this was around policy decisions, relationships and leadership. But that was being played out in the midst of the disturbing wider realities of politics, faith, prayer, God – and a weary loss of heart. As I drove home I was unable to pray until a surge of emotion welled up from my guts. For the next few miles I raged, wept, shouted and thumped the steering wheel as hard as I could (I probably should have pulled over). I completed the journey in numb silence, chest heaving, hands feeling bruised and vaguely bewildered by what had erupted inside me. I was startled and slightly afraid.

But God did not strike me down.

That evening I spent some time reflecting on what had happened and my responses. This language of prayer was new to me. I needed time to learn it. I had to begin by learning to tell the difference between separating sulking and lament, grumbling and protest, moaning and prayer. But in that raw, chaotic place I had a sense of energy and encounter with God where it was needed most.

This happens in the psalms. Prayers that begin with lament often end with deliverance and praise. 'You have turned my mourning into dancing' (Ps. 30.11). But this is much more than God giving a 'happy ending'. In fact the outward circumstances may not have changed much at all in the first instance. In the tears and passion of honest lament we meet God, and faith is forged and shaped by an improbable but stubborn hope.

Lament is the antidote to despair.

29

Water into Wine

A poem by Michael Symmons Roberts describes a bedroom the morning after a night of weeping. He pictures the room as like a shoreline, left saturated by a tide that has now receded, leaving pools and damp. Tears, he says, have 'marinated' the room. Whatever he has been weeping over, the poet now speaks to himself firmly, calling out new courage and direction. That flood of tears has left him free to choose and to act in new ways. The fears that previously inhibited him are now like gunpowder that is too damp to ignite (*Drysalter*, p. 62).

The image of tears as a marinade is original and gentle in a poem that hints at storms and flooding. The presence of gunpowder also points to the destructive capability of human emotions. By contrast, the work of a marinade is both to flavour and tenderise. In the soaking work of tears the texture of our life is softened to new responsiveness, with new flavour and essence. The transforming work of tears finds beautiful expression here.

In popular imagination the destiny we hope for in what we call heaven is a place where there will be no more tears. This is made explicit in the book of Revelation. In the new heaven and earth God 'will wipe every tear from their eyes. Death will be no more; mourning and crying and pain will be no more, for the first things have passed away' (Rev. 21.4). These are the very particular tears that are part of life in a world of much tragedy, disappointment, unhealed wounds and frustrated longing. This is good news.

But, as we have seen, tears are also an important way we respond to the joy, beauty, love and gifts in life. They are not just for pain. So it is hard to imagine a place of joyful fullness and divine beauty without having tears with which to celebrate it. Words will not be enough. We will need another language.

Maggie Ross speaks of tears as 'an earnest of the joy to come' (*The Fountain and the Furnace*, p. 196). She means that at their deepest source our tears flow from something far more than human pain or unsolved problems. Tears, even in pain and bewilderment, express a capacity to wonder and to love that is found at the heart of who we are, in God's image, sustained in his life. If we will allow them, they lead us away from ourselves into a self-forgetting humility that opens us to the fullness that is the life of God. Our tears are a marinade, immersing, soaking, preparing us for our part in the gift of something quite beyond.

In the scene of the final celebrations at the end of Tolkien's *Lord of the Rings* it suddenly dawns on Sam that all the hopes that had sustained him through the direst moments of their long and terrible journey have actually been fulfilled.

> He laughed aloud for sheer delight, and he stood up and cried: 'O great glory and splendour! And all my wishes have come true!' And then he wept. And all the host laughed and wept, and in the midst of their merriment and tears the clear voice of the minstrel rose like silver and gold, and all were hushed. And he sang to them, now in the Elven tongue, now in the speech of the West, until their hearts, wounded with sweet words, overflowed, and their joy was like swords, and they passed in thought out to regions where pain and delight flow together, and tears are the very wine of blessedness. (pp. 953-4)

Tolkien draws on his Christian faith as he uses sacramental language to speak of the tears flowing in that place of final victory and peace. For Christians the 'wine of blessedness' also reminds us of Jesus drinking from the cup of blessing at the Last Supper with his disciples and saying, 'I will never again drink of this fruit of the vine until that day when I drink it new with you in my Father's kingdom' (Matt. 26.29).

All will be transformed. Water into wine.

The new heaven and earth will surely be a place where, amid so much else beyond imagining, we will discover that all is transformed.

The tears become marinade

and water now wine.

Appendix 1

Tracing our relationship with tears

Our relationship with tears goes back to our very first moments after birth. As we grow it will have been shaped and influenced by a subtle variety of relationships and experiences, positive and negative. It may help to take time to trace some of these.

The questions below may help you to get started. There are no right or wrong answers.

If a memory associated with tears comes to mind, or tears themselves surface, try to note the 'texture' and 'feel' of what is there. For example – is a story attached to it? Is the memory welcoming or tense, fearful or trusting, warm or cold, a gift or a punishment?

If no particular memory surfaces at any point just let it be. Don't force it.

When did you last cry? *(circle as appropriate)*
Do you weep   often   occasionally   rarely?
Do tears come   easily   with difficulty   very few, if any?

What memories do you have of tears in your childhood?
Where were tears to be found (open or hidden) in your home/early life?
Who was shedding them?
How were tears received – yours and others? For example,

comfortably, embarrassedly, discouragingly/in silence etc?

What was your experience of tears at school/with friends and social group?

When people see you crying what do you believe they are thinking of you?

What has been the place of tears in your spiritual journey – church or elsewhere?

Are you generally comfortable or uneasy with the tears of others?

Do you ever wish you could cry and cannot?
If so, are there other ways you express what you are feeling?

Are tears around in moments that feel 'spiritual'?
If so, what are they generally expressing? For example, awe, fear, wonder, longing, joy, sorrow …

Are there places, times, events or activities that easily trigger your tears?
For example, a film/story, an event, music …

What response is most helpful from others when you are weeping?

Do particular stories of you and tears come to mind?

If you could summarise your relationship with tears in two sentences what would you say?

Take time to reflect on what surfaces from these questions. There is no hurry. Some may find it helpful to talk through their answers with a friend.

Appendix 2

The names we call our tears

We use a very wide variety of names and words for tears. Exploring them will help us understand our relationship to tears – our own and others.

From the list in the box on page 129 pick out the words that are part of your own vocabulary for talking about and describing tears – your tears or those of others.Add any other words you use that are not on this list.

Tears occur in very different contexts. Our choice of words will reflect this to some degree. So do not worry if your list seems a bit contradictory. For example, the words describing weeping in public may well be different from words we use to describe tears shed alone.

The words and names listed in the box variously express: embarrassment, scorn, mockery, sexism, playfulness or teasing. Some are simply descriptive. We can describe our tears with varying levels of drama ('The flood gates opened'). We use lots of similes and metaphors, from 'rivers' to 'burst pipes' or 'like a baby'.

The same word can be heard as scornful and mocking when spoken by one person but as affectionate and caring when spoken by another. Context, relationship and tone of voice are all important. Is the difference always clearly heard by you?

Memories or stories may come to mind as you sift through these words. If they do, allow them to surface and listen to them. Ask yourself how they illustrate your relationship to tears. They have surfaced for a reason.

Reviewing our language for tears

Do your more regular words for tears tend to be more caring or judgmental, accepting or critical, loving or rejecting? Notice if this changes according to situation and context.

Are there words on this list that suggest other ways of naming, expressing or describing your tears? For example, if you have become aware your choice of words tends to be more negative and judging are there more caring and supportive words you could replace them with? If your words are simply descriptive, could you select words that invite more playful, imaginative and reflective ways of expressing what is happening?

In the light of this reflection:

- Is there anything you wish to pray for?
- Would it help to seek out the discernment of others for what you are discovering?

Words for tears

crying

cracking up   breaking down   filling up

a tissues moment

shedding   choking up

losing it

bawling my eyes out   weeping   drowning in...

brimmy

howling   blubbing

welling up   snivelling

cry baby   sobbing

crying bitterly   soppy   teary moment

getting emotional

the dam burst

well of tears

being a girl

being a sissy

turning on the water works

turning on the taps

going soggy

being a baby   shedding

having a good cry   making an exhibition of myself

falling apart   in floods of tears

Appendix 3

Listening to our tears

Throughout this book there have been stories and examples of tears and our relationship to them. By way of summary, here are some suggestions for seeking to listen and respond to our tears when they come.

If nothing particular surfaces in response to these suggestions do not try to force insights to appear. Be gentle. Simply let the tears be present and flow as they will.

Accept. There will of course be circumstances when it is not helpful or appropriate for our tears to surface, though it may not stop them from trying! When that happens we will need ways of 'holding them in' or seeking somewhere private. But, where possible, accept your tears when they arrive. Do not try to hide, judge or suppress them.

Ask. Talk to your tears as gently and trustingly as you are able. They may well have a story or message. 'Please tell me about these tears.' 'Help me understand.'

Sense. Is there any particular mood to your tears? Do they have a texture: for example, soft, hard, heavy or fragile? Are particular feelings present with them: for example, anger, joy, despair, longing ?

Associations and memories. Are particular stories, or memories surfacing with these tears? Just notice them. Sometimes tears come with a message: for example, 'I am lost', 'I am lonely', 'I long for ...'

When there are no tears. Please see the suggestions in Chapter 4.

'Stuck' tears. Some tears have a sense of going nowhere. We weep without a sense of anything being resolved, as if we are just circling around something. This may suggest unresolved or unhealed issues in our lives. Or something seeking to be understood that so far eludes us. This is a place where some may find it a help to seek the wisdom of a supportive listener. Listening to ourselves can often be harder than listening to others.

Counselling and support. This book explores some of our deepest human responses, often out of our deepest needs and longings. For this very reason I encourage readers to be open to seeking further guidance and support where this would be helpful.

References

Alter, Robert, *Genesis*, New York: W. W. Norton & Co., 1996.

Alter, Robert, *The Book of Psalms*, New York: W. W. Norton & Co., 2007.

Alter, Robert, *The David Story*, New York: W. W. Norton & Co., 1999.

Bannatyne, Duncan, *Anyone Can Do It*, London: Orion Books, 2006.

Barrington-Ward, Simon, *The Jesus Prayer*, London: BRF, 1996.

Belton, Neil, *The Good Listener – Helen Bamber: A Life against Cruelty*, London: Weidenfield & Nicholson, 1998.

Bourdieu, Pierre, *Bourdieu: A Critical Reader*, ed. Richard Shus terman, Oxford: Blackwell, 1999.

Bowler, Kate, 'Wishing Job's Comforters Well', *Church Times*, 16 February 2018.

Brand, Russell, https://relevantmagazine.com/feature/the-second-coming-of-russell-brand/.

Brown, Raymond, *The Gospel According to John: Vol. 1*, Anchor Bible, New York: Continuum, 1971.

Brueggemann, Walter, *The Message of the Psalms*, Minneapolis, MN: Augsburg, 1984.

Buechner, Frederick,www.frederickbuechner.com/listening-to-your-life/.

Campbell, Dennis, 'Facebook and Twitter harm young people's mental health', *The Guardian*, 19 May 2017.

Center for Action and Contemplation: https://cac.org/science-week-2-summary-2015-11-14/.

Chamorro-Premuzic, Tomas and Lusk, Derek, 'The Dark Side of Resilience', *Harvard Business Review*, August 2017.

Coakley, Sarah, *The Cross and the Transformation of Desire: The Drama of Love and Betrayal*, Cambridge: Grove Books, 2014.

Compassion Fatigue Awareness Project, www.compassionfatigue.org.

Cotter, Jim, *By Stony Paths: A Version of Psalms 51–100*, Norwich: Cairns Publications, 1991.

Cottrell, Bishop Stephen, sermon preached at the consecration of two new bishops in St Paul's Cathedral, 25 January 2012. Full text available at www.salisbury.anglican.org/news/bishop-john-wraw-consecrated.

Cushman, Philip, www.nytimes.com/1995/03/31/books/books-of-the-times-the-self-and-those-who-tend-it.html.

de Caussade, Jean Pierre, *Abandonment to the Divine Providence*, San Ramon, CA: Vision Press, 2018.

Dostoevsky, Fyodor, *The Brothers Karamazov*, Ware: Wordsworth Edition, 1987.

Draycott, Andy, http://ccca.biola.edu/advent/2017/#day-dec-16.

Eadie, Donald, *A Grain in Winter*, London: Epworth, 1999.

Estes, Clarissa, *Women Who Run with Wolves*, London: Rider & Co., 1998.

Everplans, www.everplans.com/articles/5-things-you-need-to-know-about-direct-cremation.

Fisher, Rose-Lynn, *The Topography of Tears*, New York: Bellevue Literary Press, 2017. To see some of her photos go to http://rose-lynnfisher.com/tears.html.

Foster, Richard, *Prayer: Finding the Heart's True Home*, London: Hodder & Stoughton, 2008.

Francis, Leslie, www.churchtimes.co.uk/articles/2014/7-

february/ features/features/do-we-have-the-right-class-of-bishop.

Frank, Anne, *Diary of Anne Frank*. London: Pan, 1968.

Frankl, Victor, quoted in Walter Brueggemann, *The Message of the Psalms*, Minneapolis, MN: Augsburg, 1984.

Grubb, Norman, *Rees Howells: Intercessor*, Fort Washington, PA: CLC Publications, 2016.

Harmless, William, *Desert Christians: An Introduction to the Literature of Early Monasticism*, Oxford: Oxford University Press, 2004. For a helpful summary of tears in the desert tradition, see: www.patheos.com/blogs/billykangas/2011/05/the-role-of-tears-in-the-spiritual-life-lessons-from-the-desert-fathers.html.

Hauerwas, Stanley, 'The Servant Community', in *The Hauerwas Reader*, ed. John Berkman and Michael Cartwright, Durham, NC: Duke University Press, 2001.

Heath, Elaine, *The Mystic Way of Evangelism*, Ada, MI: Baker Academic, 2017.

Holden, Anthony and Holden, Ben (ed.), *Poems that Make Grown Men Cry*, London: Simon & Schuster, 2015.

Hollenweger, Walter, *The Pentecostals*, London: SCM Press, 2012.

Ineson, Mat, personal communication. Quoted with grateful thanks.

Jarral, Farrah, https://www.bbc.co.uk/programmes/b09wg6gp.

Kay, John, *Obliquity: Why Our Goals are Best Achieved Indirectly*, London: Profile Books, 2011.

Kempe, Margery, *The Book of Margery of Kempe*, London: Penguin Classics, 2008.

Kendrick, Graham, 'My true feelings', from the album *The Breaking of the Dawn*, Dovetail, 1976.

Kreider, Alan, *The Patient Ferment of the Early Church: The*

Improbable Rise of Christianity in the Roman Empire, Grand Rapids, MI: Baker Academic, 2016.

Lewis, C. S., *The Four Loves*, San Diego, CA: Harcourt Brace, 1991.

Liguori, Alphonsus de (1696–1787), quoted in *Duties and Dignities of the Priest*, ed. Eugene Grimm, Brooklyn, NY: Redemptorist Fathers, 1927.

Macfarlane, Robert, *The Wild Places*, London: Granta, 2007.

Magdalene, Margaret, *Furnace of the Heart*, London: Darton, Longman & Todd, 1998.

McNeill, Donald, Morrison, Douglas, Nouwen, Henri, *Compassion*, London: Darton, Longman & Todd, 1982.

Michaels, Ann, *Fugitive Pieces*, New York: Continuum, 2009.

Millard, Rosie, www.independent.co.uk/voices/im-glad-people-including-david-bowie-are-starting-to-opt-for-direct-cremation-funerals-are-outdated-a6939516.html.

Mingana, Alphonse, quoting Joseph the Seer (born c. 710), in *Early Christian Mystics*, Piscataway, NJ: Gorgias Press LLC, 2012.

Monastery, see, for example: *The Big Silence*, Tiger Aspect, DVD, 2011; *Bad Habits*, www.channel5.com/show/bad-habits-holy-orders/.

Nouwen, Henri, *The Genesee Diary*, New York: Bantam Doubleday, 1981.

Ó Tuama, Padraig, *In the Shelter: Finding a Home in the World*, London: Hodder & Stoughton, 2015.

Orr, Deborah, 'I used to think people made rational decisions', www.theguardian.com/commentisfree/2017/dec/28/second-thoughts-rational-decisions-brexit-trump.

Parke, Simon, www.churchtimes.co.uk/articles/2004/25-june/comment/tasting-the-sweets-of-surrender.

Polen, Rabbi Nehemia '"Sealing the Book with Tears": Divine

Weeping on Mount Nebo and in the Warsaw Ghetto', in Kimberley Patton and John Hawley (eds), *Holy Tears: Weeping in the Religious Imagination*, Princeton, NJ: Princeton Books, 2005.

Raymo, Chet, *The Soul of the Night: An Astronomical Pilgrimage*, Upper Saddle River, NJ: Prentice Hall Direct, 1985.

Rishawy, Derek, https://mereorthodoxy.com/beauty-impassible-god-god-emotional-teenager/.

Roberts, Michael Symmons, *Dysalter*, London: Jonathan Cape, 2013.

Ross, Maggie, *The Fountain and the Furnace: The Way of Tears and Fire*, Eugene, OR: Wipf and Stock, 2014. Ross's book remains the only theological study of tears that I am aware of. It is a demanding read but I am indebted to it's insights.

Rumi, 'The Edge of the Roof', in *The Rumi Collection: An Anthology of Translations of Mevlâna Jalâluddin Rumi*, Boulder, CO: Shambhala Publications Inc., 2004.

Runcorn, David, *Space for God: Silence and Contemplation in the Christian Life*, Darton, Longman & Todd, 1990.

Ryrie, Alec, *Being Protestant in Reformation Britain*, Oxford: Oxford University Press, 2013.

Shade, JoAnn, https://www.cbeinternational.org/resources/article/other/immersed-tears.

Sheldon, Julie, *The Blessing of Tears,* Norwich: Canterbury Press, 2004.

Sheldrake, Philip, *Befriending Your Desires*, London: Darton, Longman & Todd, 1998.

Symmons Roberts, Michael, 'Portrait of the Psalmist as a man in tears', in *Drysalter*, London: Cape Poetry, 2013.

Tamaro, Susanna, www.azquotes.com/author/18109-Susanna_Tamaro.

Tear bottles: www.lachrymatory.com/History.htm.

The Message: The Bible in Contemporary Language, Colorado Springs, CO: Nav Press, 2009.

Thomas, Simon, https://agriefshared.com.

Tolkien, J. R. R., *The Lord of the Rings*, New York: Houghton Mifflin, 1954.

United States Geological Survey: https://water.usgs.gov/edu/propertyyou.html.

Ware, Kallistos, *The Orthodox Way*, New York: St Vladimir's Seminary Press, 1998.

Watts, Isaac, 'O God our help in ages past', *Hymns Ancient and Modern Revised*, Norwich: Canterbury Press, 1983.

Whyte, David, *Crossing the Unknown Sea: Work and the Shaping of Identity*, London: Penguin 2001.

Whyte, David, www.davidwhyte.com/the-heart-aroused/. Published as *The Heart Aroused: Poetry and the Preservation of the Corporate Soul of America*, New York: Bantam Doubleday Dell Publishing Group, 1996.

Wright, Christopher, *The Book of Lamentations*, London: InterVarsity Press, 2015.

Further reading

Byers, Michele and Lavery, David (eds), *On the Verge of Tears: Why Movies, Art, Popular Culture and the Real World Make Us Cry*, Newcastle upon Tyne: Cambridge Scholars Publishing, 2010.

Fisher, Rose-Lynn, *The Topography of Tears*, New York: Bellevue Literary Press, 2017. See also her website: http://rose-lynnfisher.com/tears.html

Frey II, William, *Crying: The Mystery of Tears*, Minneapolis: MN, Winston Press, 1985.

Kottler, Jeffrey, *The Language of Tears*, San Francisco: CA, Josey-Bass Inc., 1996.

Lutz, Tom, *Crying: The Natural and Cultural History of Tears*, New York: W. W. Norton & Co., 1999.

Patton, Kimberley and Hawley, John (eds), *Holy Tears: Weeping in the Religious Imagination*, Princeton, NJ: Princeton Paperback, 2005.

Ross, Maggie, *The Fountain and the Furnace: The Way of Tears and of Fire*, Eugene, OR: Wipf and Stock, 2014.

Shelton, Julie, *The Blessing of Tears*, Norwich: Canterbury Press, 2004.

Trimble, Michael, *Why Humans Like to Cry*, Oxford: Oxford University Press, 2012.